MUTTS

A Shtinky Little Christmas

PATRICK McDONNELL

Andrews McMeel
Publishing, LLC
Kansas City · Sydney · London

MUTTS is distributed internationally by King Features Syndicate, Inc. For information, write to King Features Syndicate, Inc., 300 West Fifty-Seventh Street, New York, New York 10019 or visit www.KingFeatures.com.

Andrews McMeel Publishing, LLC
an Andrews McMeel Universal company
1130 Walnut Street, Kansas City, Missouri 64106

12 13 14 15 16 SDB 10 9 8 7 6 5 4 3 2 1

ISBN: 978-1-4494-2307-0

Library of Congress Control Number: 2012936736

MUTTS can be found on the Internet at www.muttscomics.com

Original coloring by Brendan Burford
Cover and text design by Jeff Schulz / Menagerie Co.

ATTENTION: SCHOOLS AND BUSINESSES
Andrews McMeel books are available at quantity discounts with
bulk purchase for educational, business, or sales promotional use.
For information, please e-mail the Andrews McMeel Publishing
Special Sales Department: specialsales@amuniversal.com.

MIX
Paper from
responsible sources
FSC® C101537
www.fsc.org

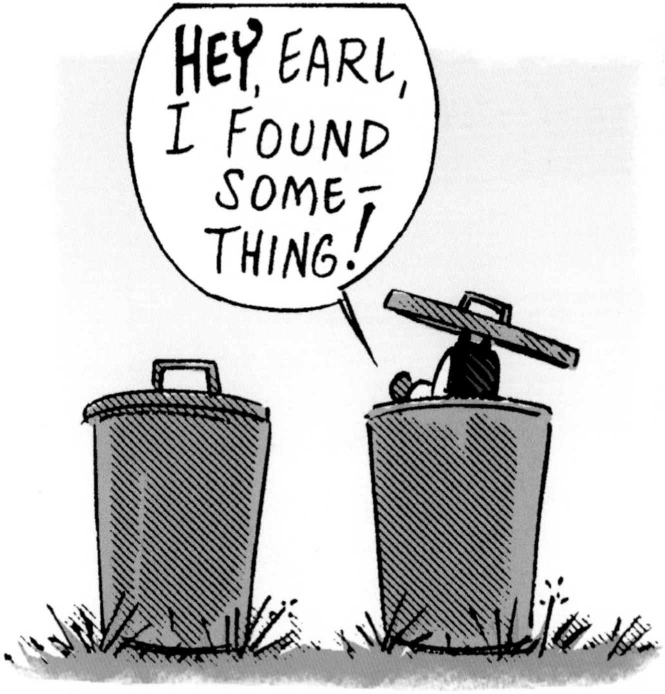
HEY, EARL, I FOUND SOME-THING!

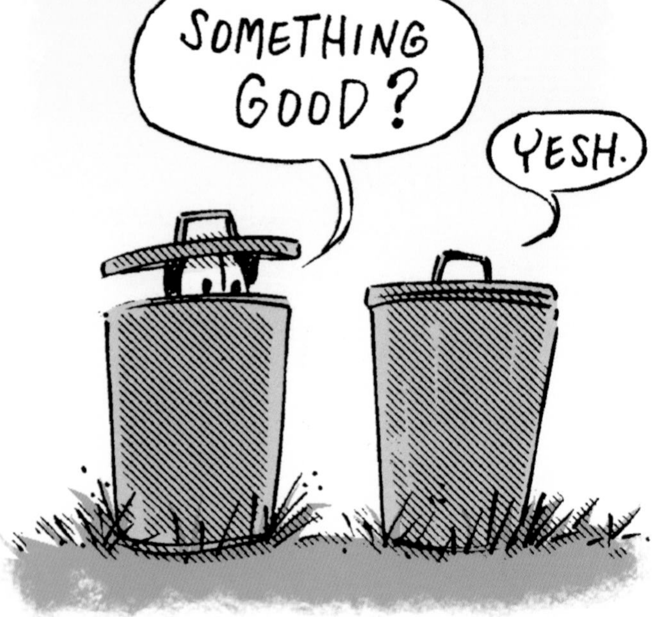
SOMETHING GOOD?
YESH.

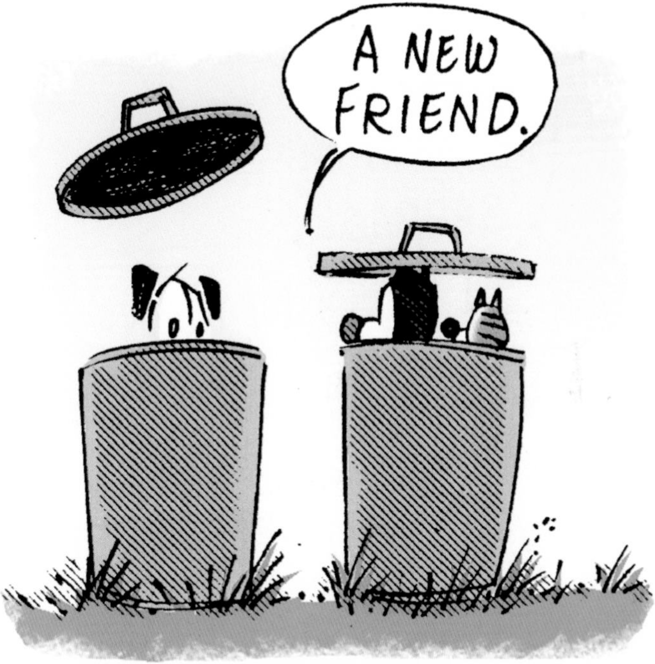
A NEW FRIEND.

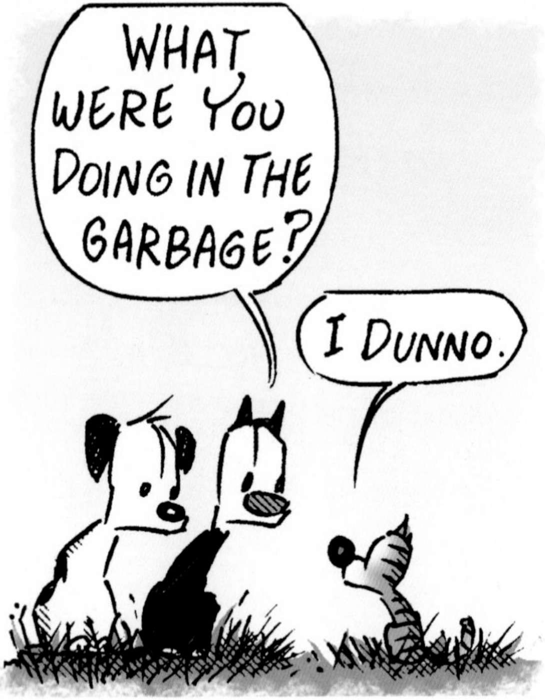
WHAT WERE YOU DOING IN THE GARBAGE?
I DUNNO.

WHAT'S YOUR NAME?
I DUNNO.
WHERE DO YOU LIVE?
I DUNNO.
WHAT'S THE MATTER WITH YOU?
I DUNNO.

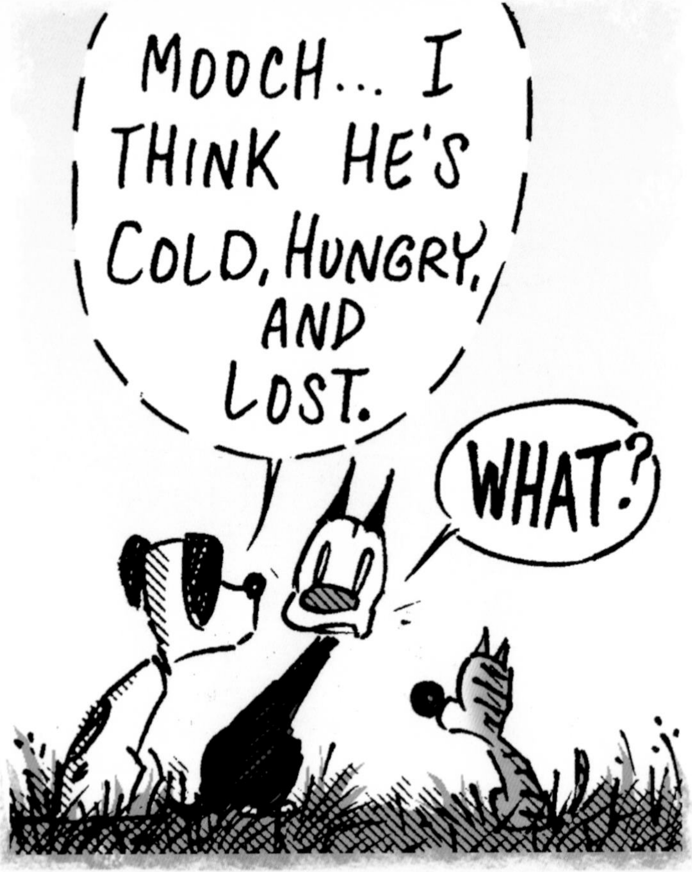
MOOCH... I THINK HE'S COLD, HUNGRY, AND LOST.
WHAT?

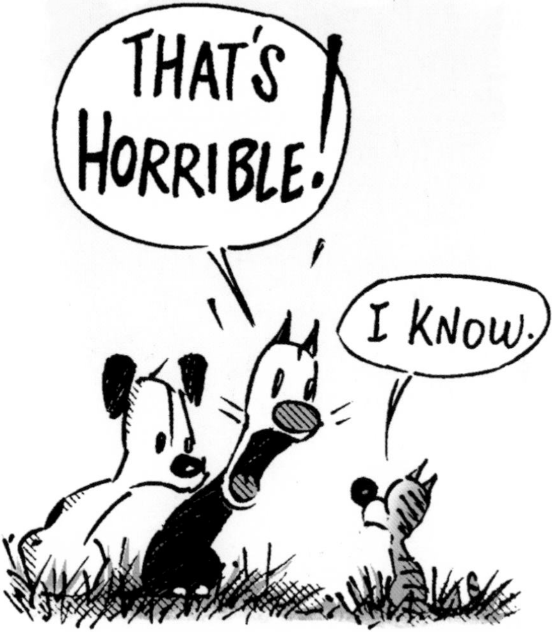
THAT'S HORRIBLE!
I KNOW.

WELL, IT LOOKS LIKE WE FOUND A LITTLE ORPHAN KITTY IN THE GARBAGE.
YESH.

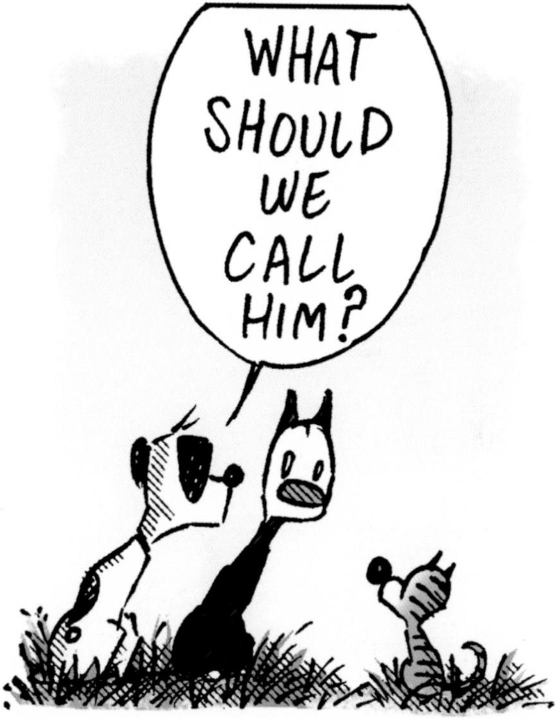
WHAT SHOULD WE CALL HIM?

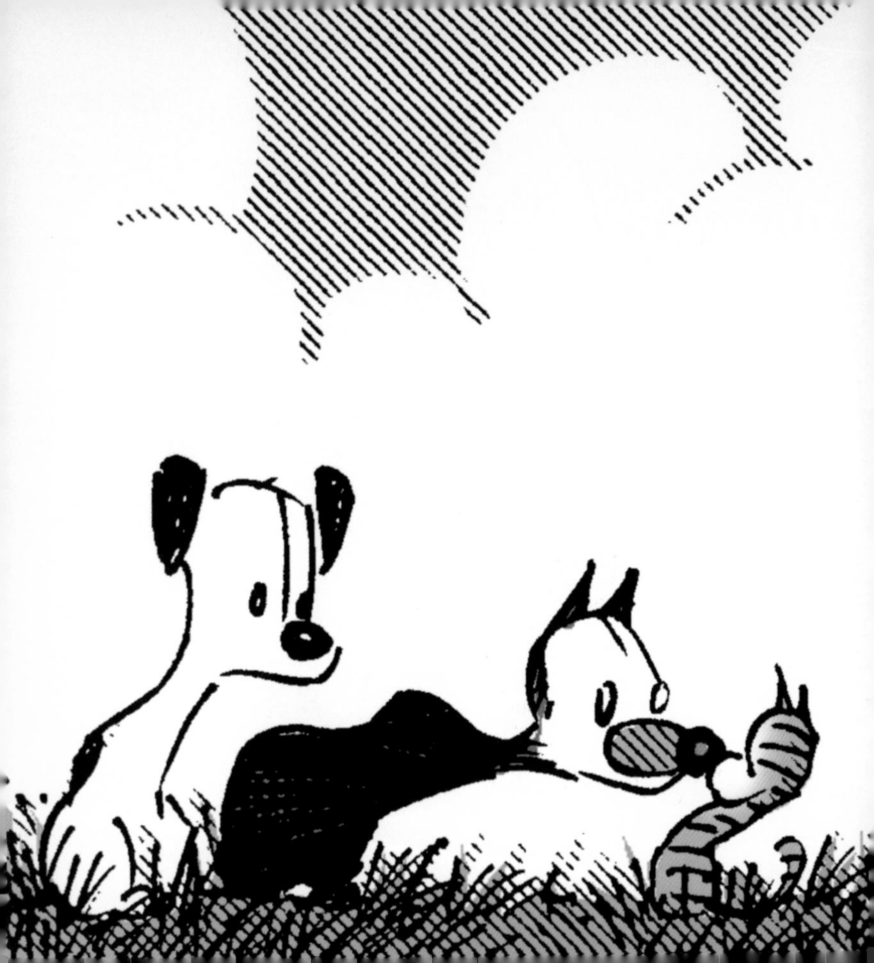

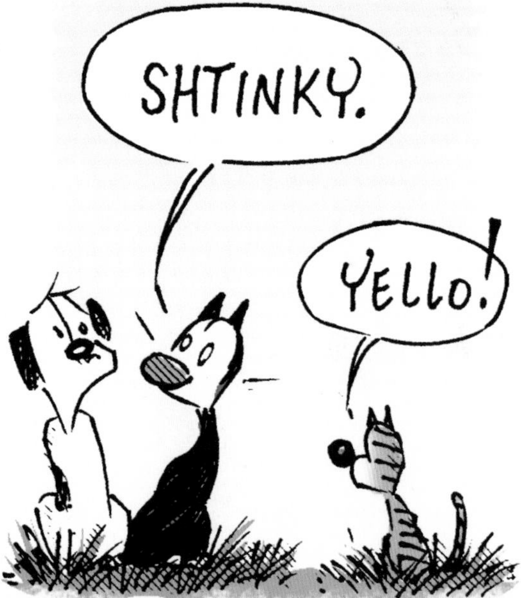
SHTINKY.
YELLO!

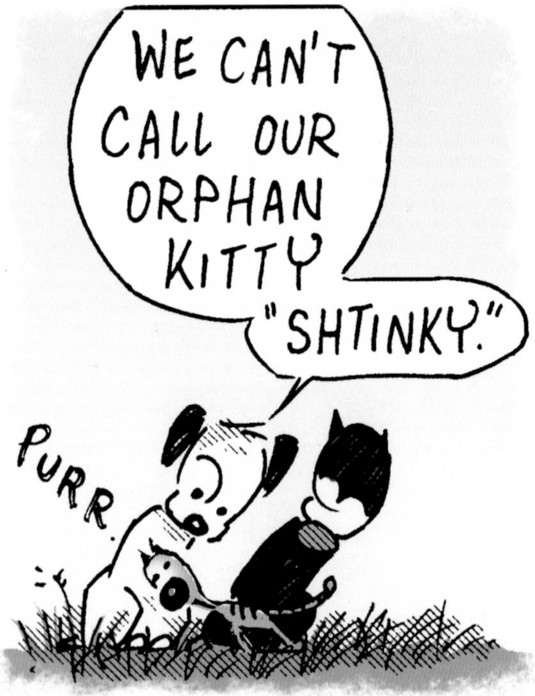
WE CAN'T CALL OUR ORPHAN KITTY "SHTINKY."
PURR.

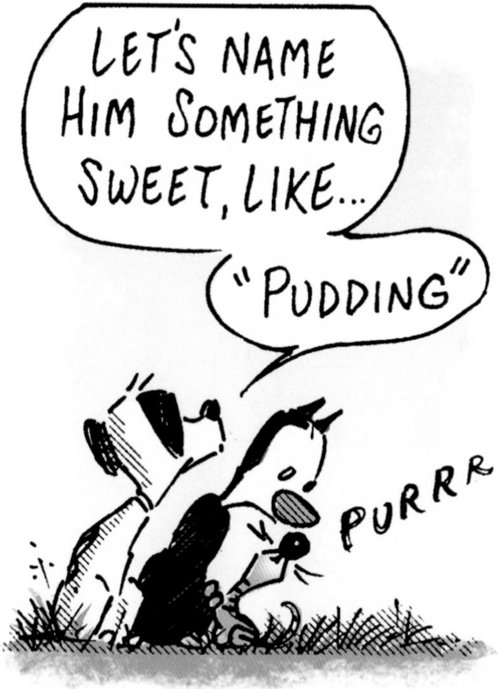
LET'S NAME HIM SOMETHING SWEET, LIKE...
"PUDDING"
PURRR

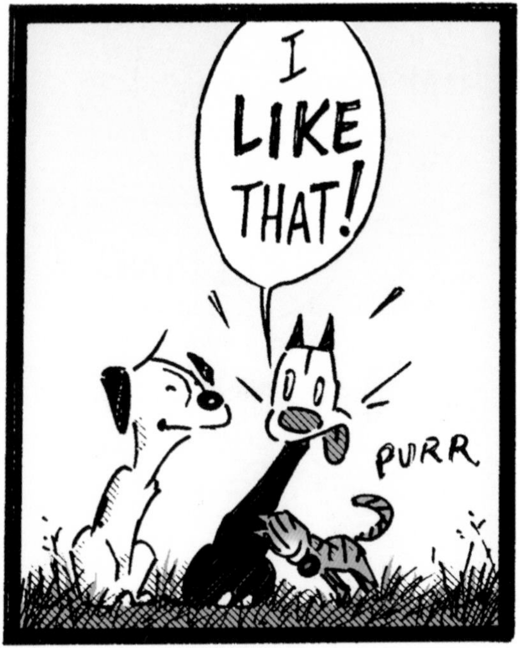
I LIKE THAT!
PURR

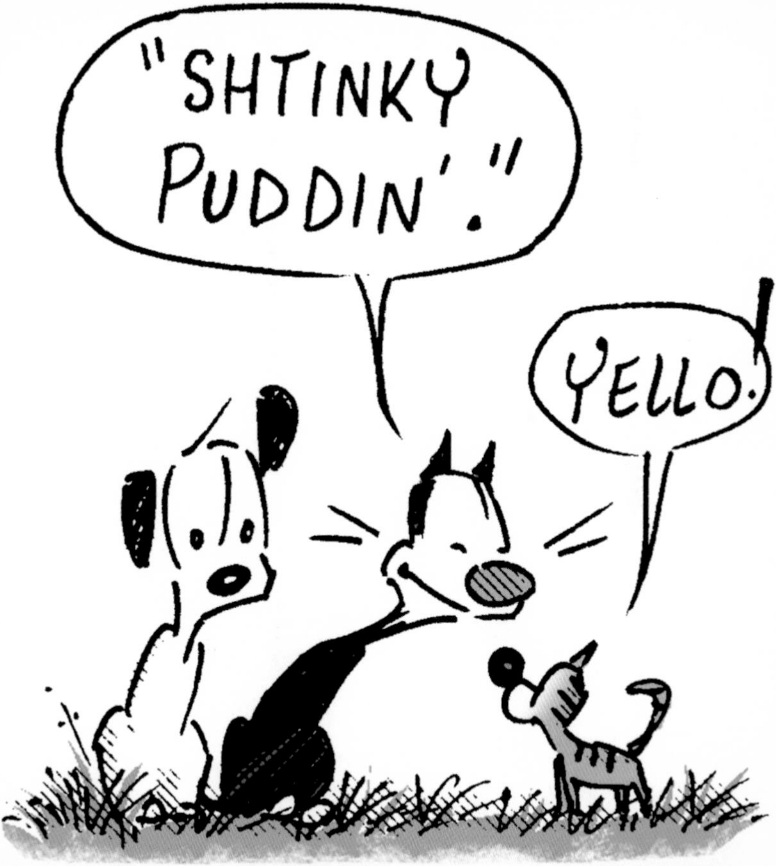
"SHTINKY PUDDIN'."
YELLO!

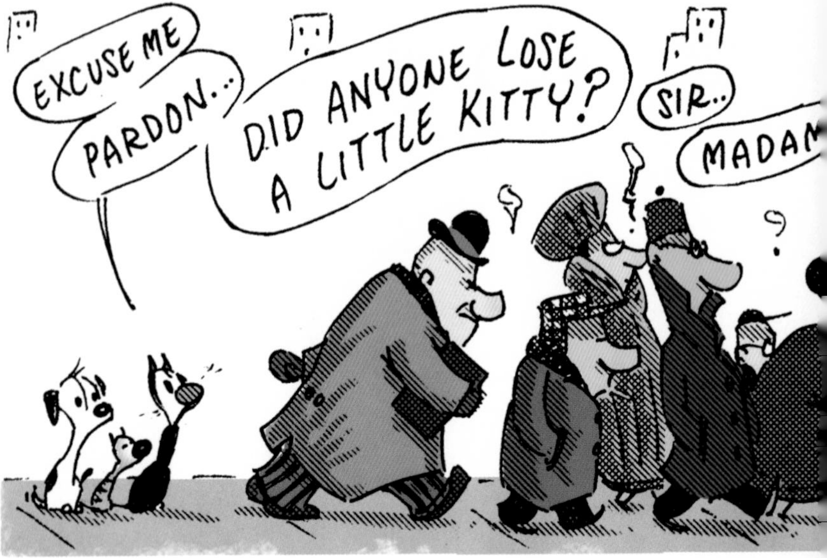
EXCUSE ME
PARDON...
DID ANYONE LOSE A LITTLE KITTY?
SIR..
MADAM

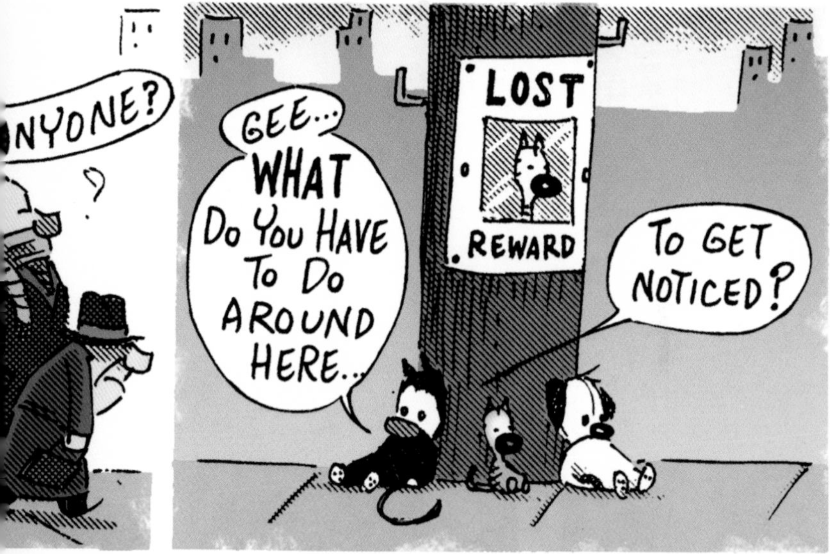
NYONE?
GEE... WHAT DO YOU HAVE TO DO AROUND HERE...
LOST
REWARD
TO GET NOTICED?

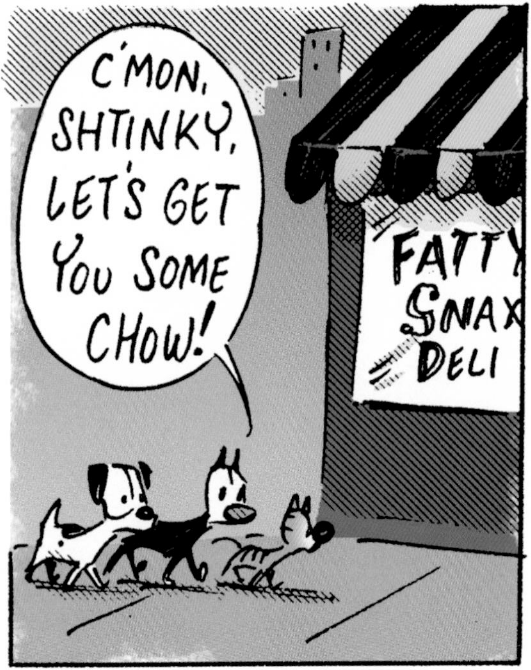
C'MON, SHTINKY, LET'S GET YOU SOME CHOW!
FATTY SNAX DELI

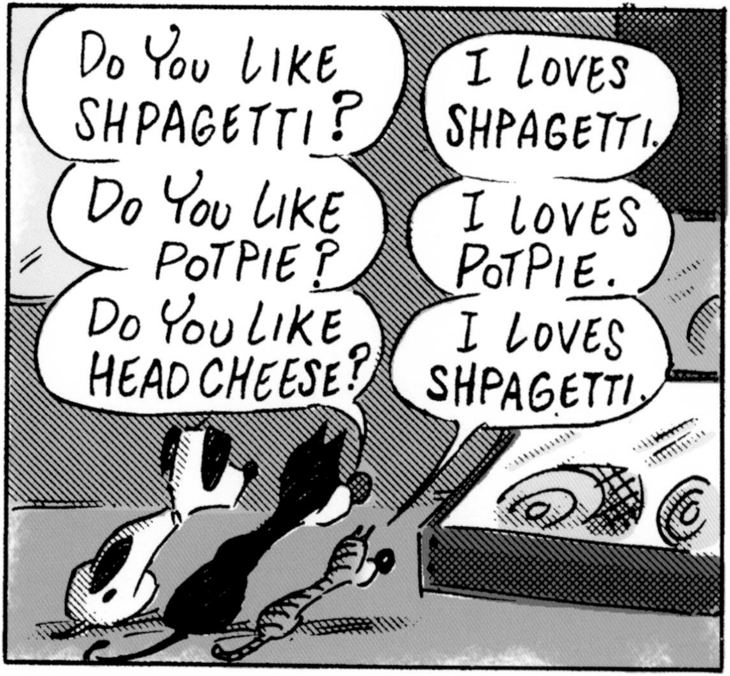
DO YOU LIKE SHPAGETTI?
I LOVES SHPAGETTI.
DO YOU LIKE POTPIE?
I LOVES POTPIE.
DO YOU LIKE HEAD CHEESE?
I LOVES SHPAGETTI.

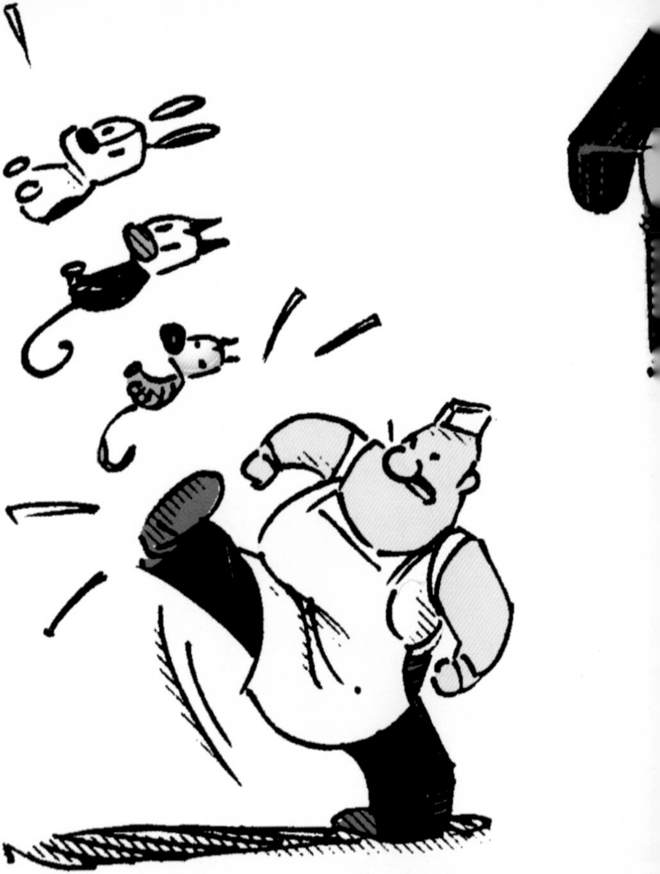

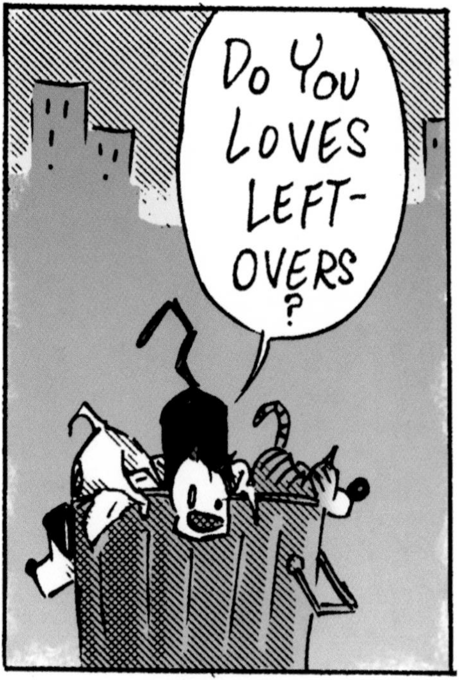
DO YOU LOVES LEFT-OVERS?

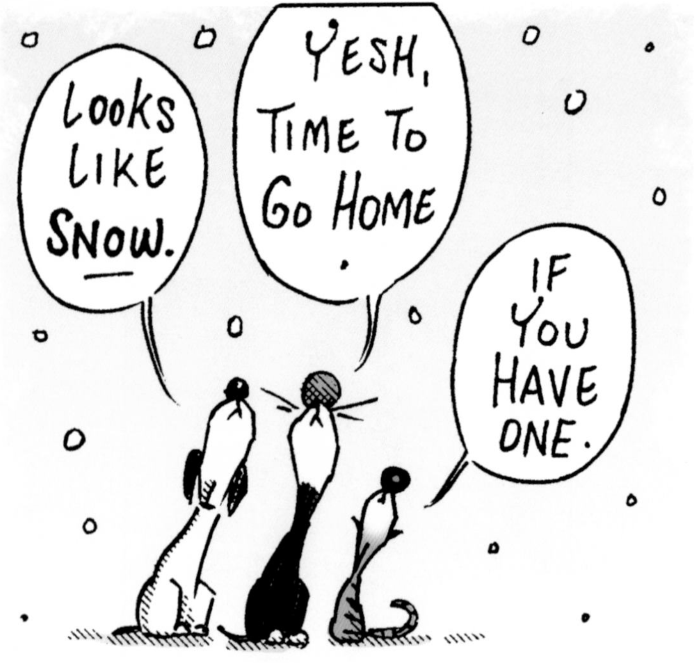
LOOKS LIKE SNOW.
YESH, TIME TO GO HOME.
IF YOU HAVE ONE.

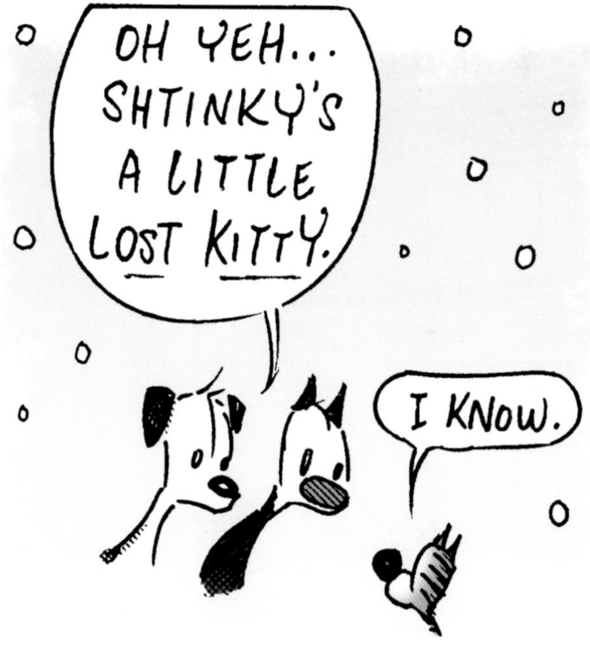
OH YEH... SHTINKY'S A LITTLE LOST KITTY.
I KNOW.

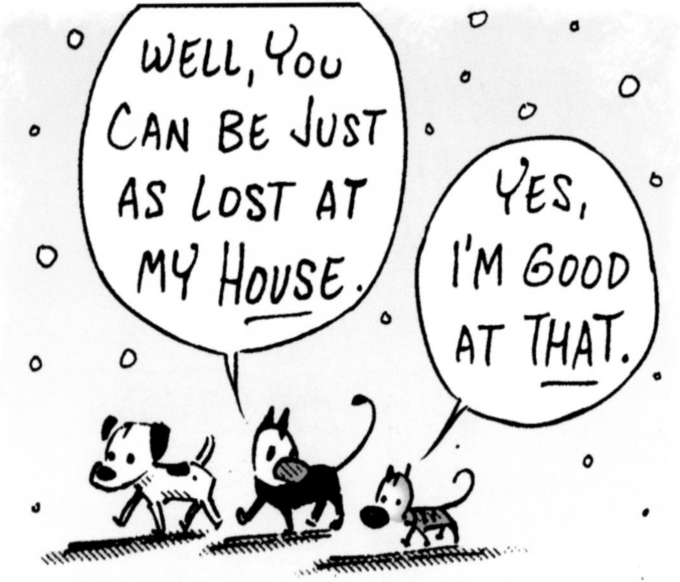
WELL, YOU CAN BE JUST AS LOST AT MY HOUSE.
YES, I'M GOOD AT THAT.

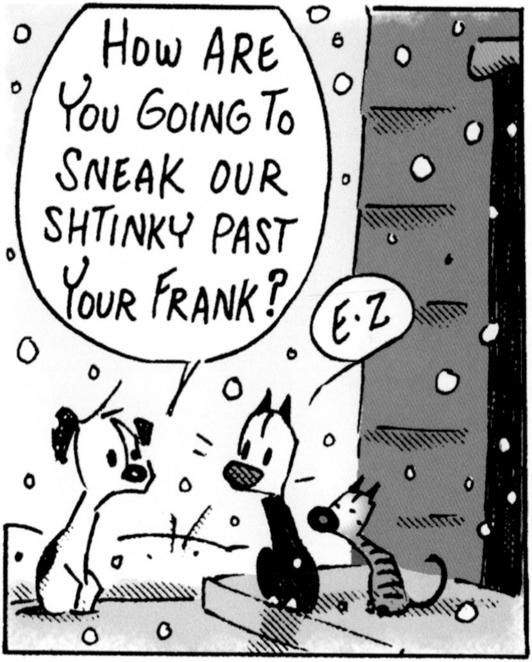
HOW ARE YOU GOING TO SNEAK OUR SHTINKY PAST YOUR FRANK?
E·Z

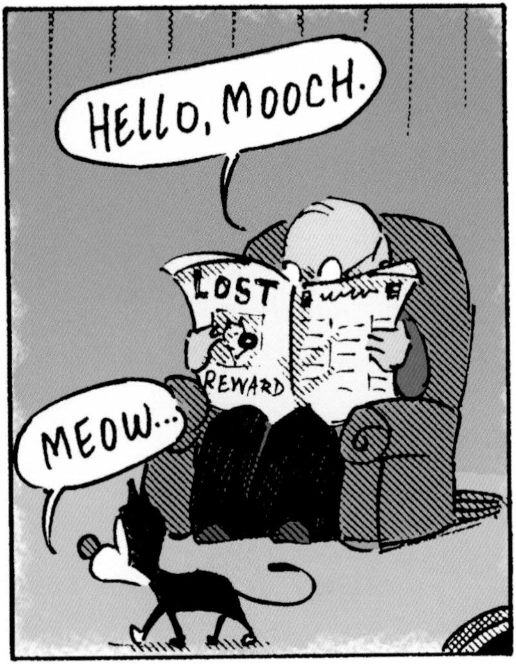
HELLO, MOOCH.
LOST
REWARD
MEOW...

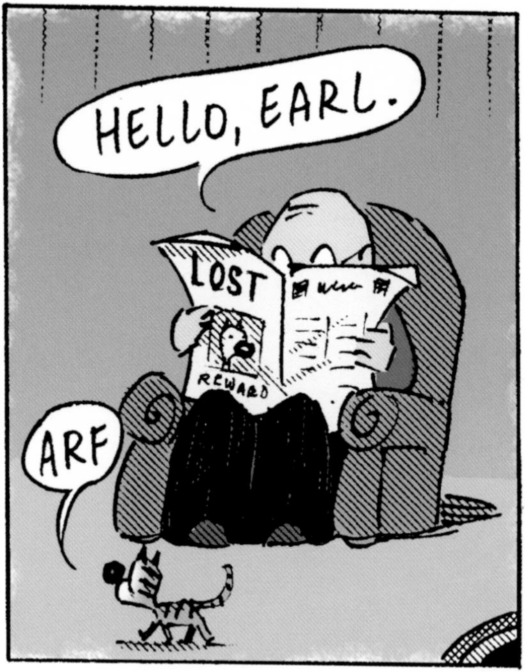
HELLO, EARL.
LOST
REWARD
ARF

Haverstraw King's Daughters Public Library

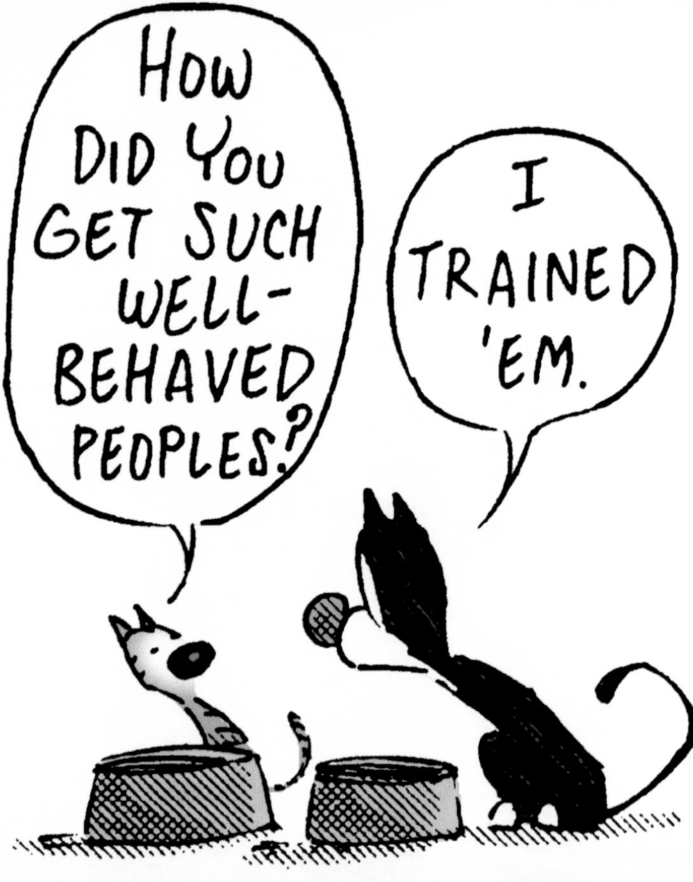
HOW DID YOU GET SUCH WELL-BEHAVED PEOPLES?
I TRAINED 'EM.

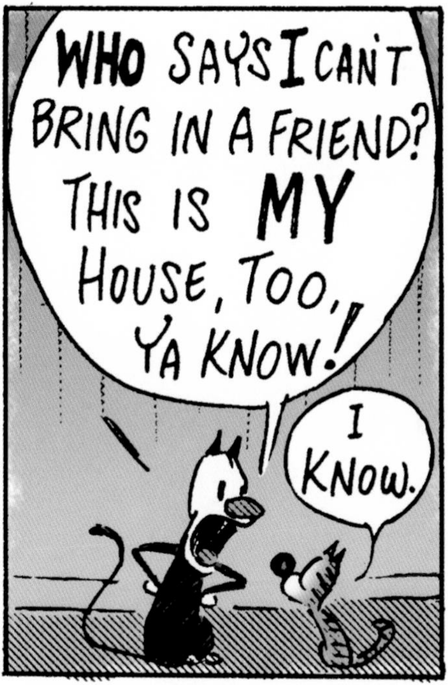
WHO SAYS I CAN'T BRING IN A FRIEND? THIS IS MY HOUSE, TOO, YA KNOW!
I KNOW.

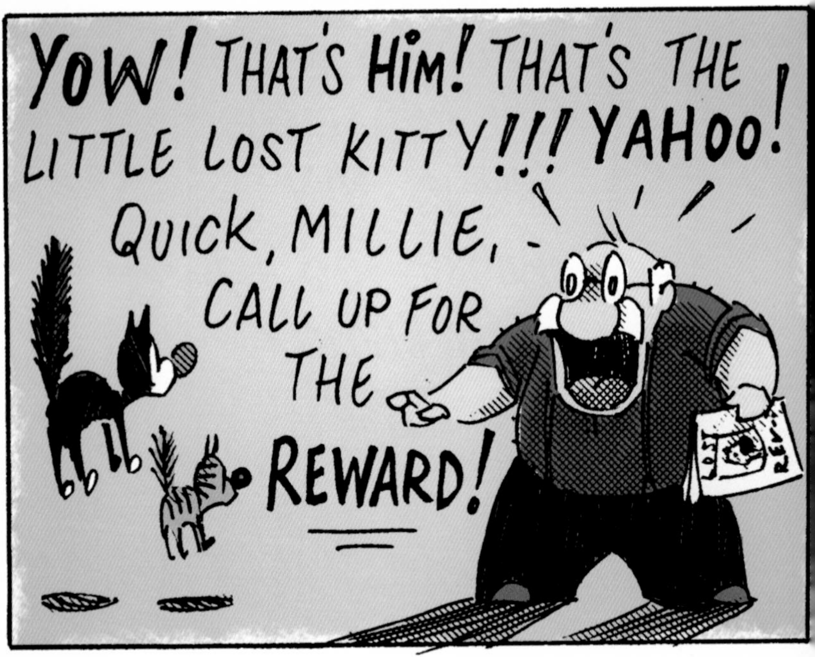
YOW! THAT'S HIM! THAT'S THE LITTLE LOST KITTY!!!! YAHOO!
QUICK, MILLIE, CALL UP FOR THE REWARD!
LOST
REW

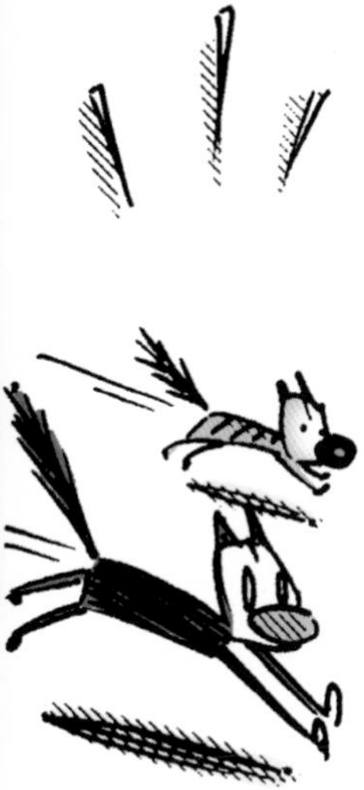

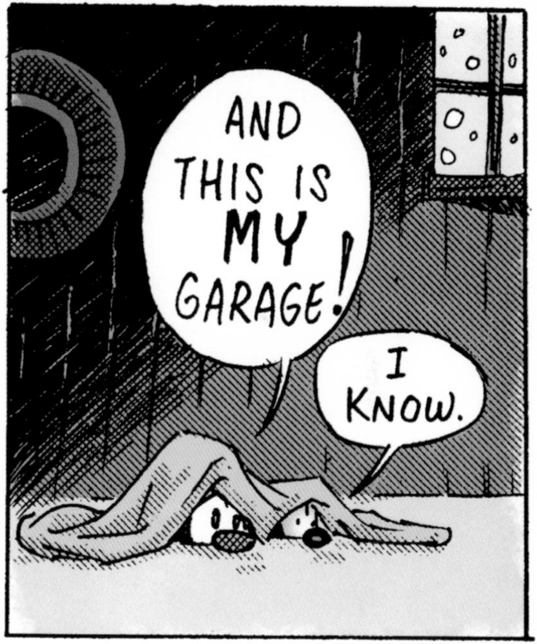
AND THIS IS MY GARAGE!
I KNOW.

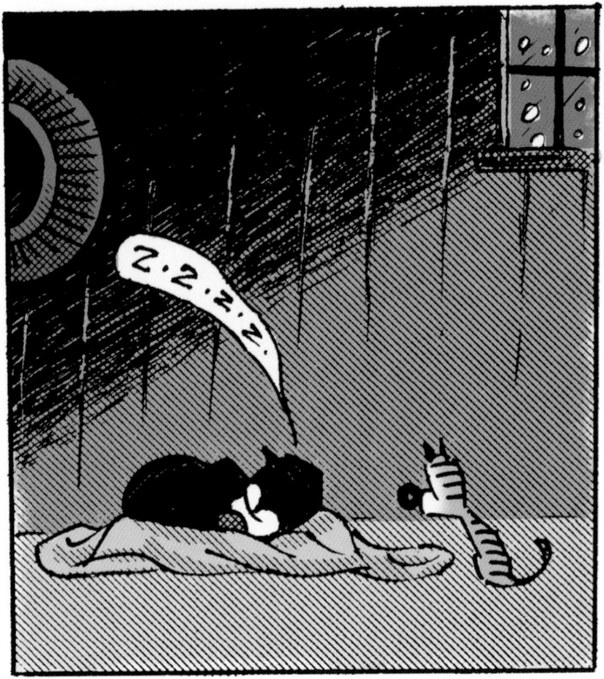
Z.Z.Z.Z.

AHH, MOOCH.
HE'S SO KIND
AND GENEROUS...
I'M NOT GOING TO
MAKE HIM A LOT
OF TROUBLE —
I'M NOT...

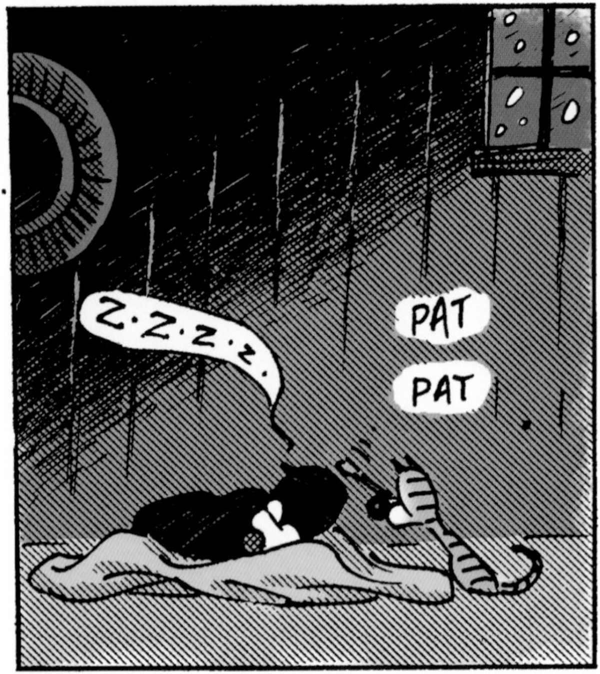
Z·Z·Z·Z·Z·
PAT
PAT

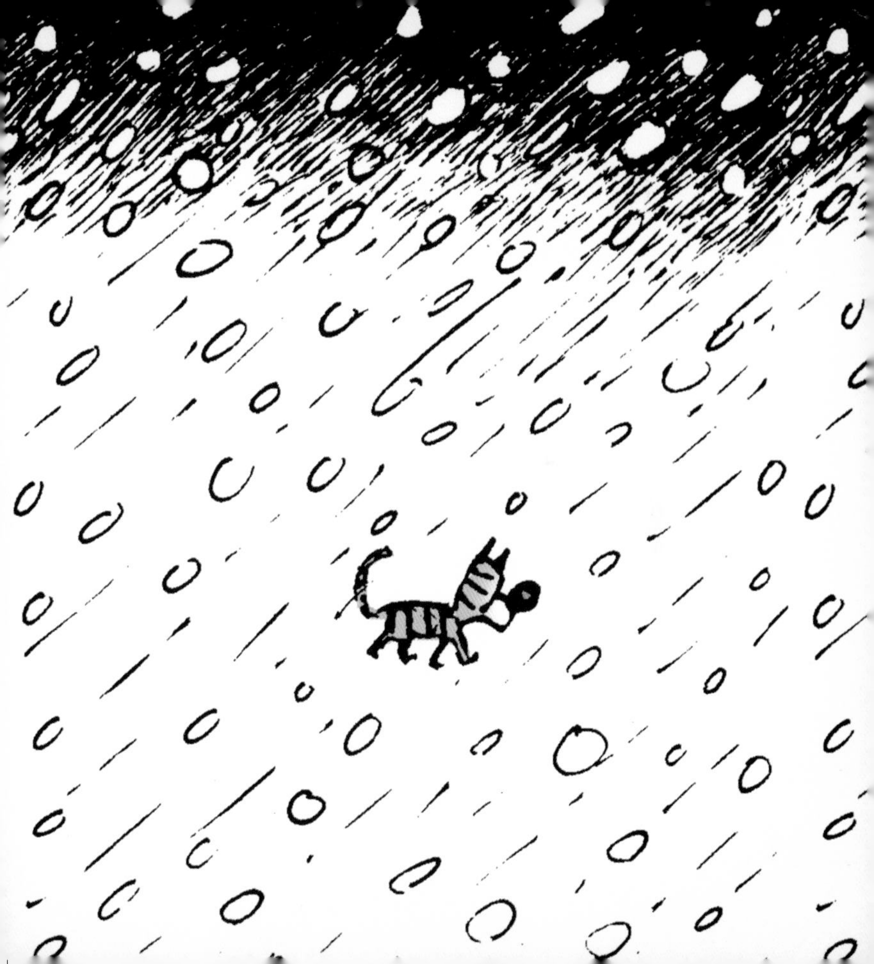

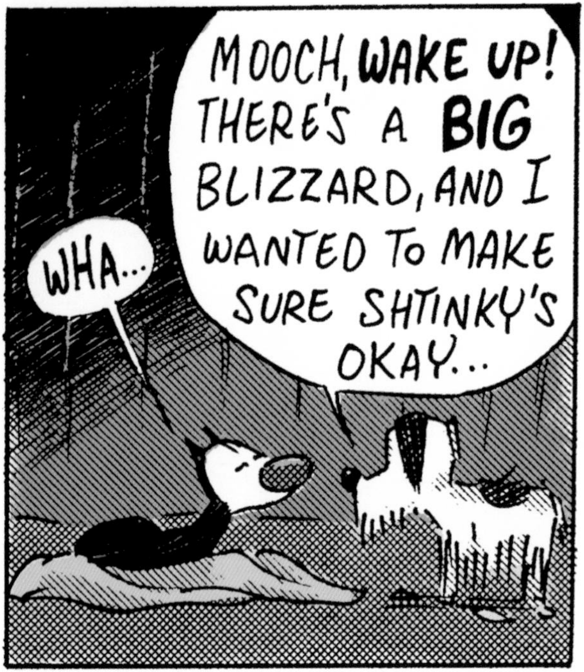
MOOCH, WAKE UP! THERE'S A BIG BLIZZARD, AND I WANTED TO MAKE SURE SHTINKY'S OKAY...
WHA...

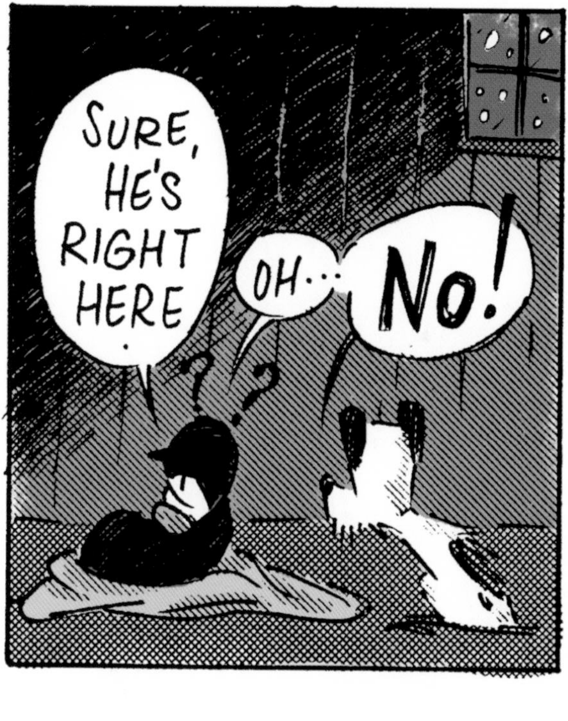
SURE, HE'S RIGHT HERE
OH...
NO!

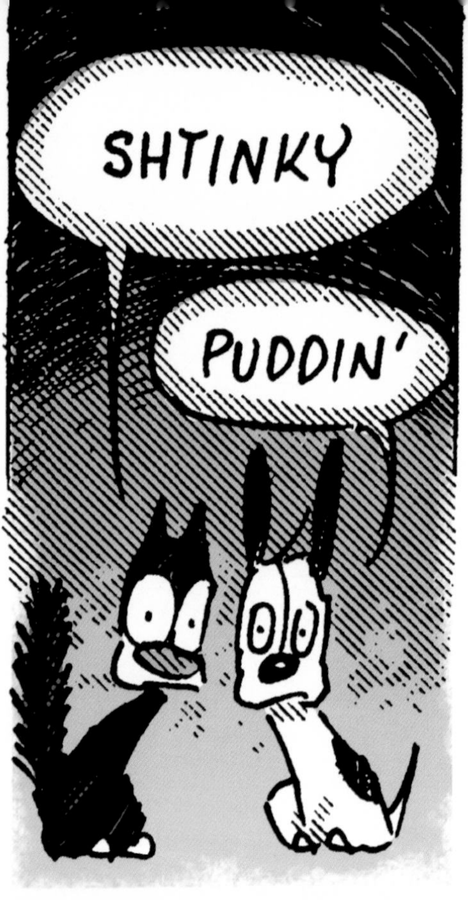
SHTINKY
PUDDIN'

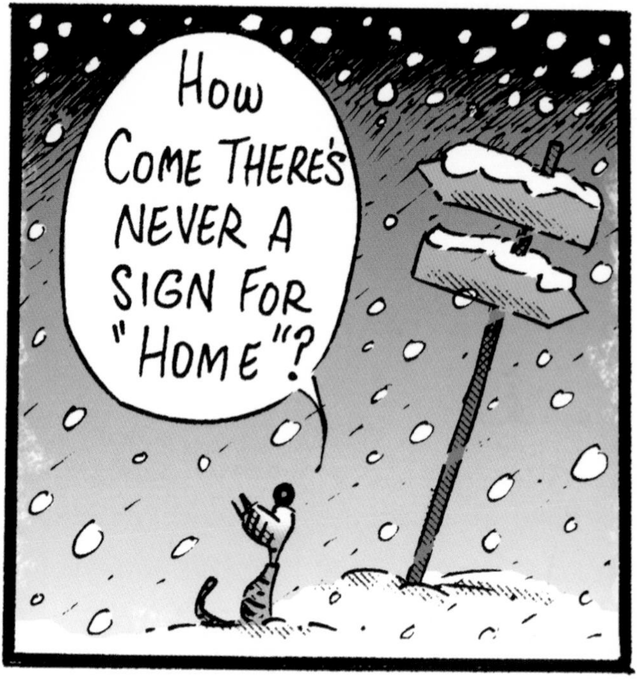
How Come There's Never a Sign for "Home"?

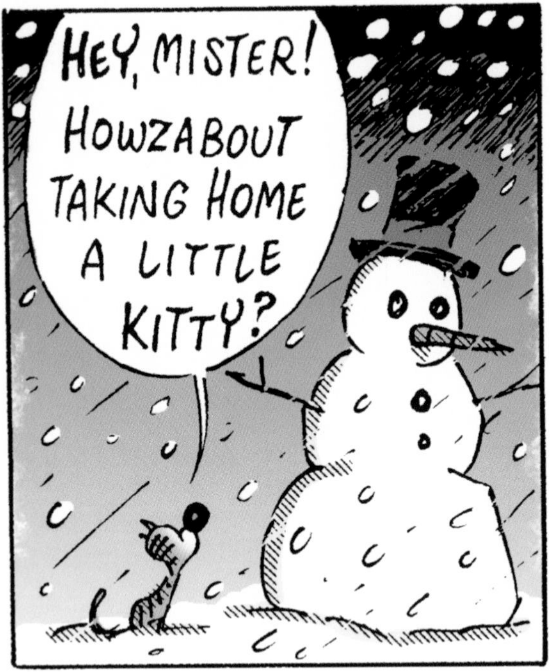
HEY, MISTER! HOWZABOUT TAKING HOME A LITTLE KITTY?

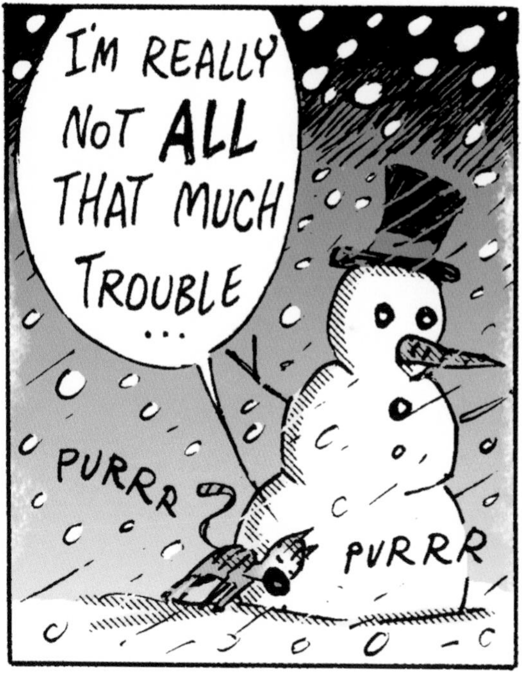
I'M REALLY NOT ALL THAT MUCH TROUBLE ...
PURRRR
PURRR

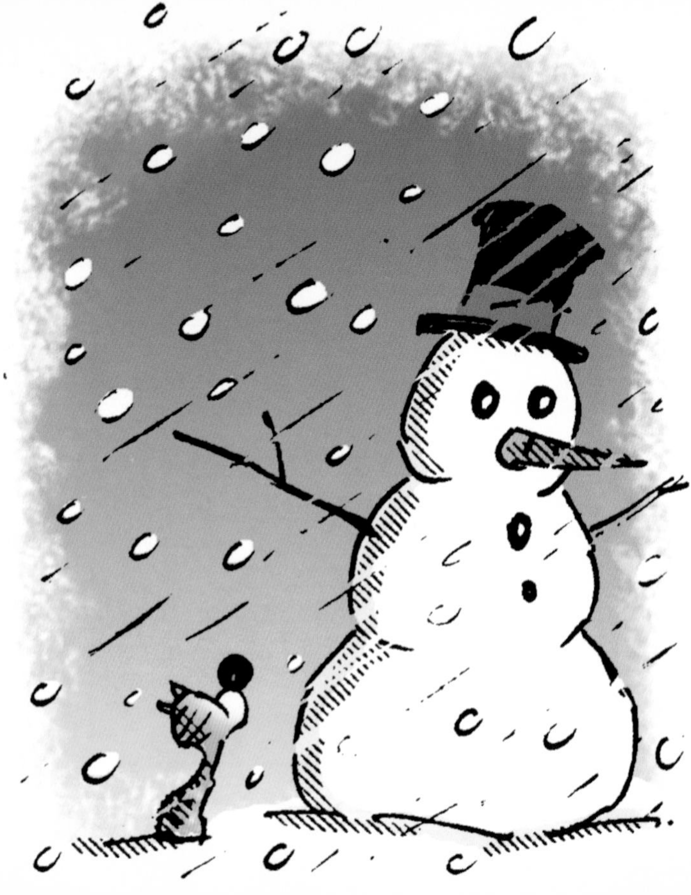

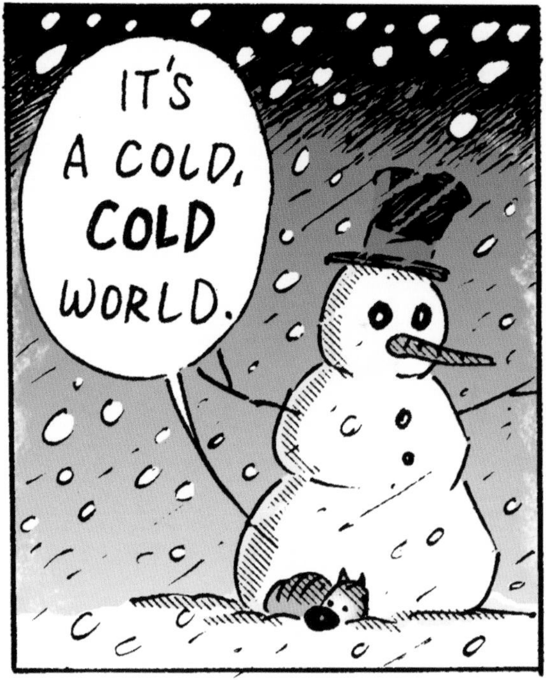
IT'S A COLD, COLD WORLD.

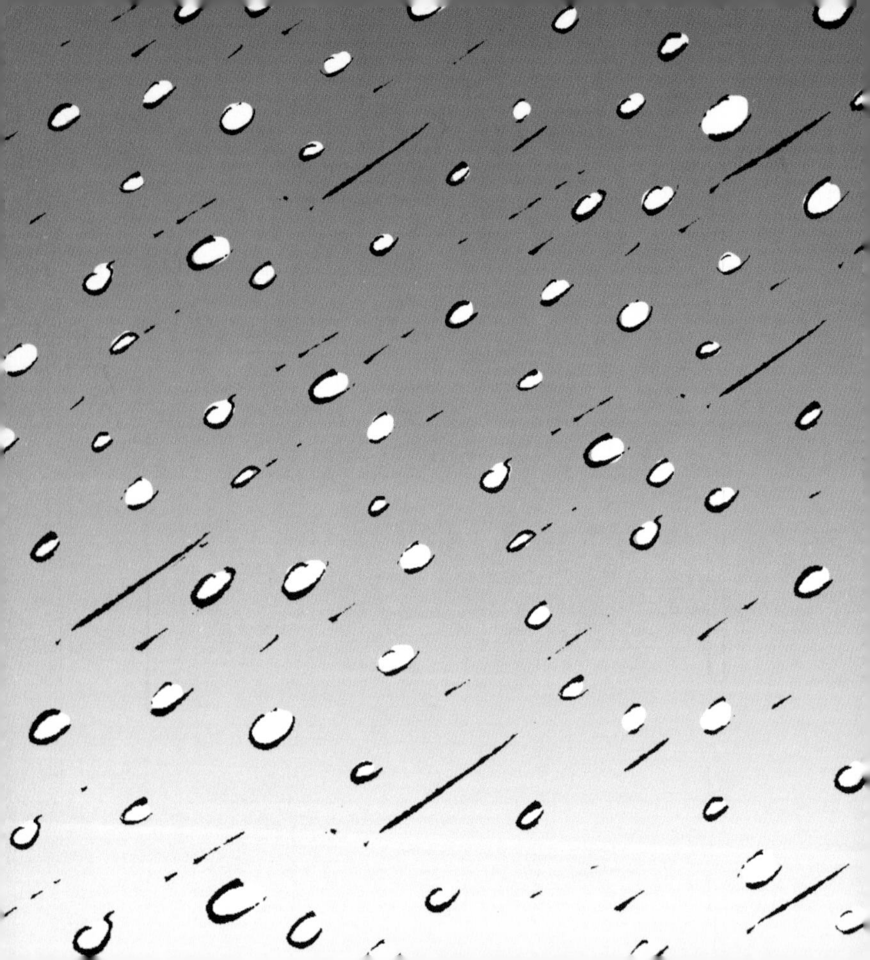

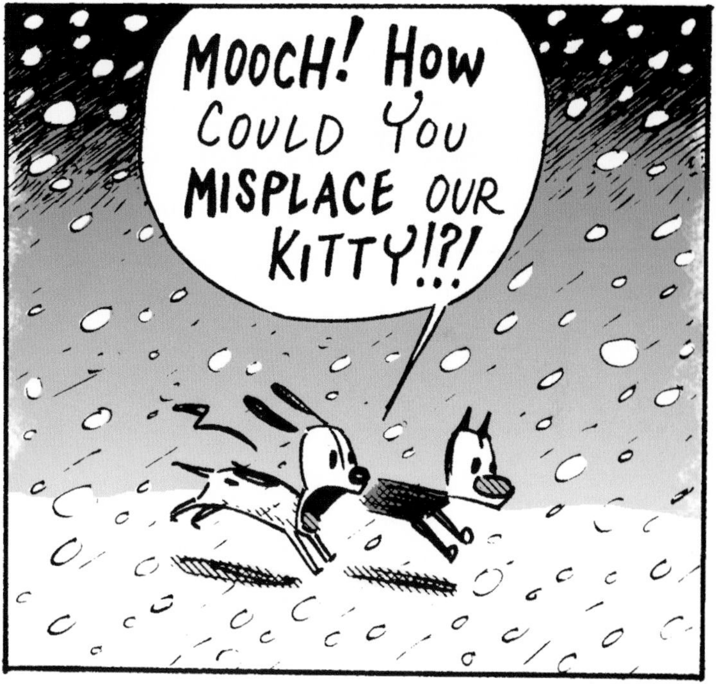
MOOCH! HOW COULD YOU MISPLACE OUR KITTY!?!

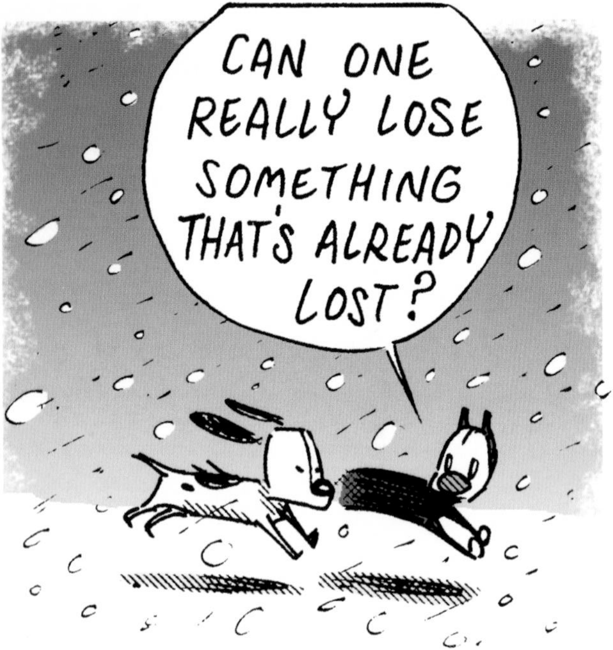
CAN ONE REALLY LOSE SOMETHING THAT'S ALREADY LOST?

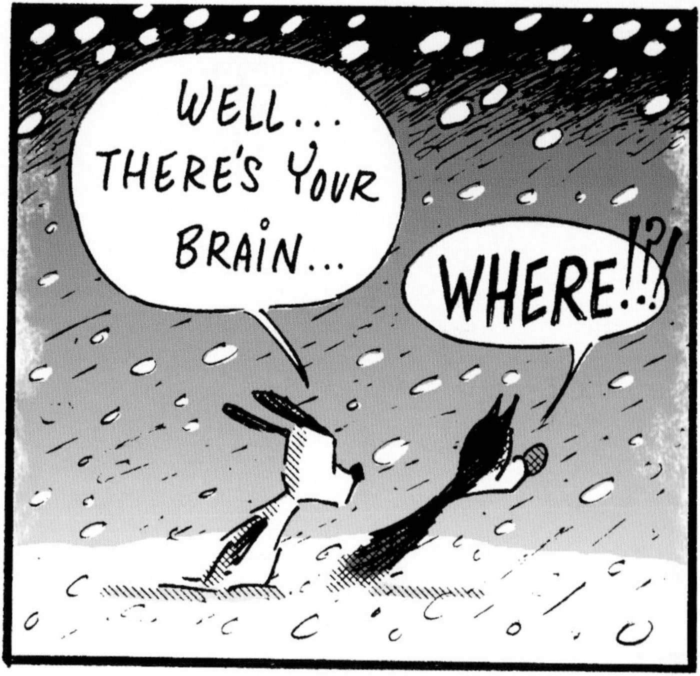
WELL... THERE'S YOUR BRAIN...
WHERE!?!

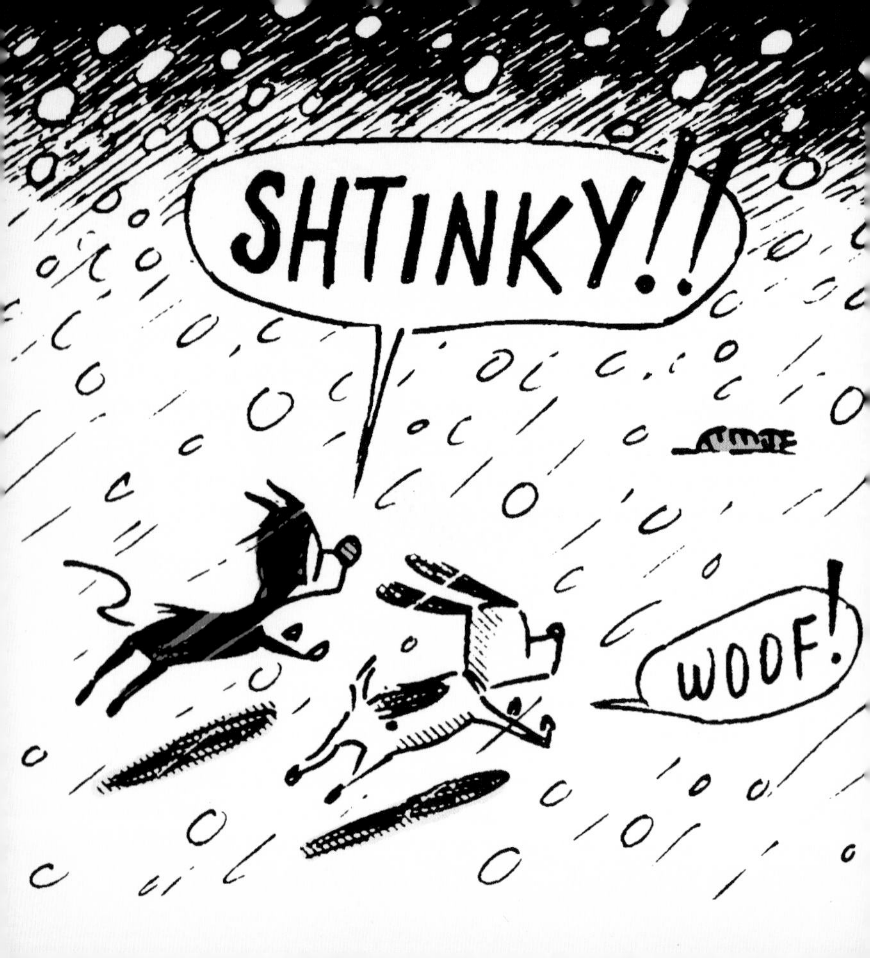
SHTINKY!!
WOOF!

WE WERE WORRIED SICK ABOUT YOU!
I KNOW.
YOU COULD CATCH A DEATH OF COLD!
I KNOW.
YOU WERE SAFE WITH US!
I KNOW.

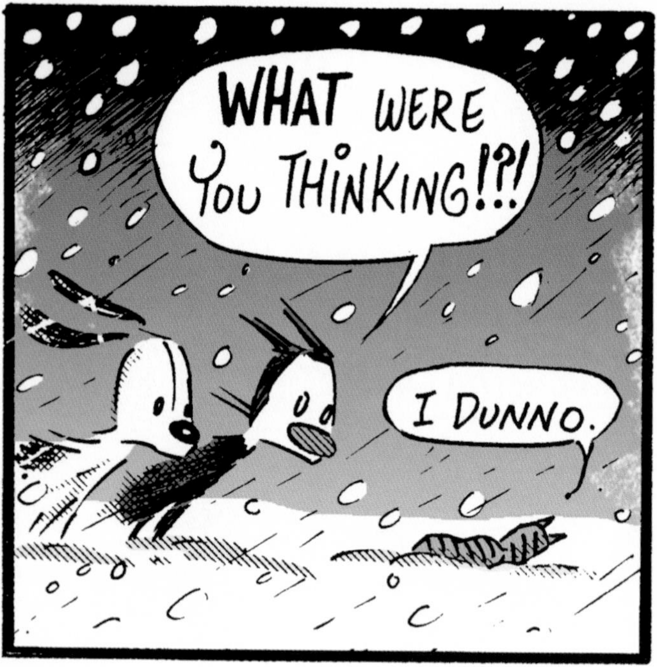
WHAT WERE YOU THINKING!?!
I DUNNO.

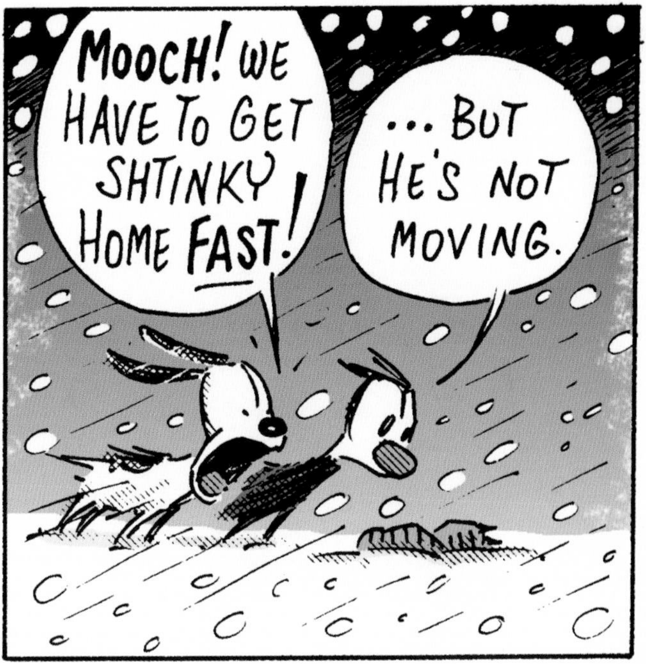
MOOCH! WE HAVE TO GET SHTINKY HOME FAST!
...BUT HE'S NOT MOVING.

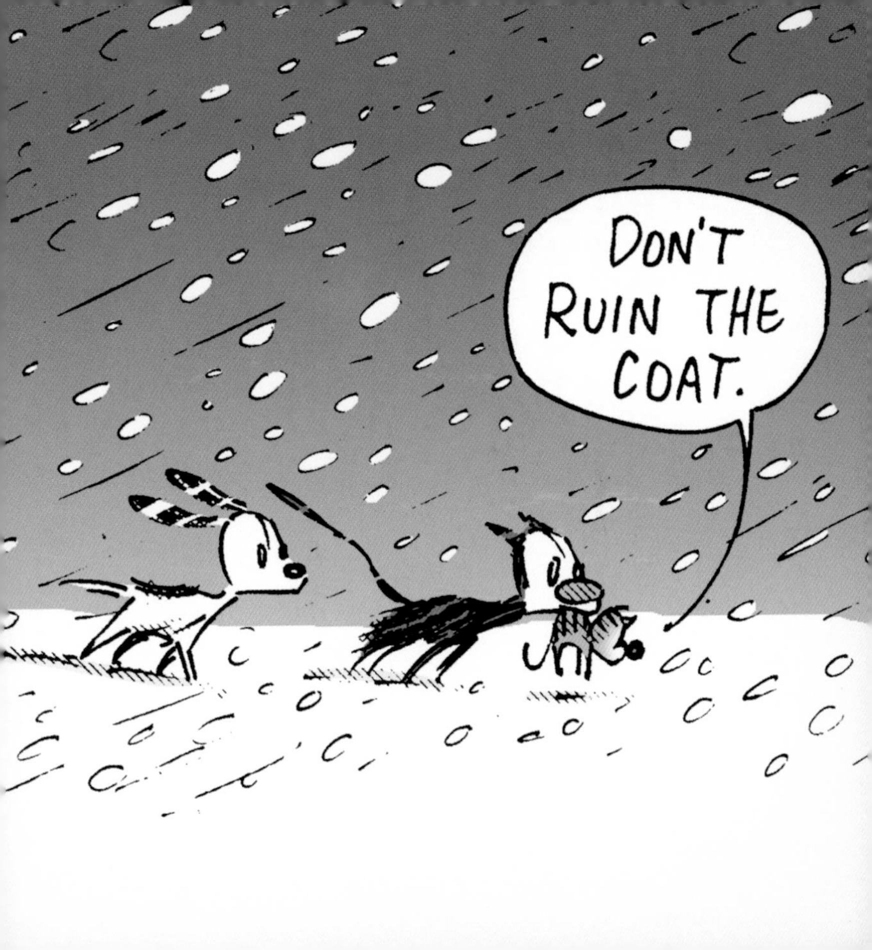
DON'T RUIN THE COAT.

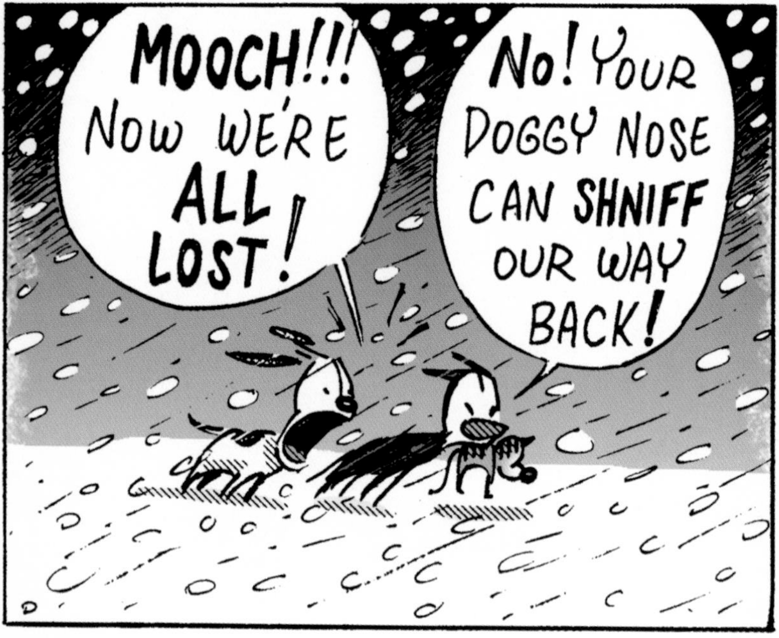
MOOCH!!! NOW WE'RE ALL LOST!
NO! YOUR DOGGY NOSE CAN SHNIFF OUR WAY BACK!

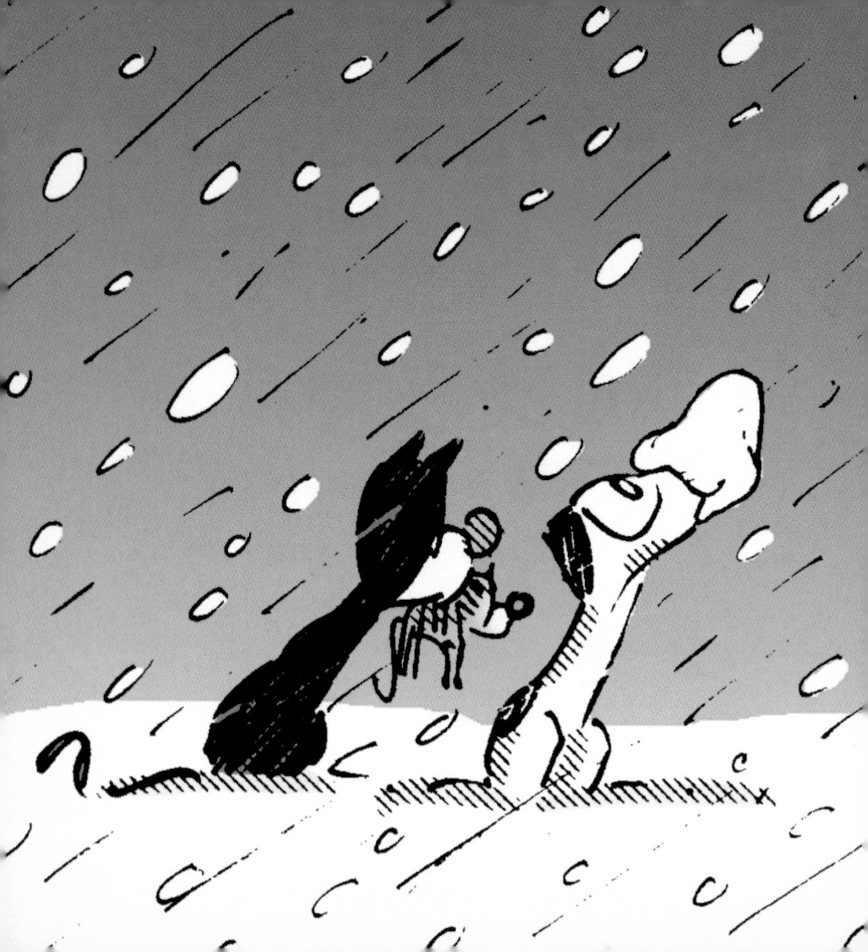

SHMAYBE SOMEONE WILL SAVE US...
HUH!?! WHAT OTHER NUT WOULD BE OUT ON A NIGHT LIKE THIS!?!

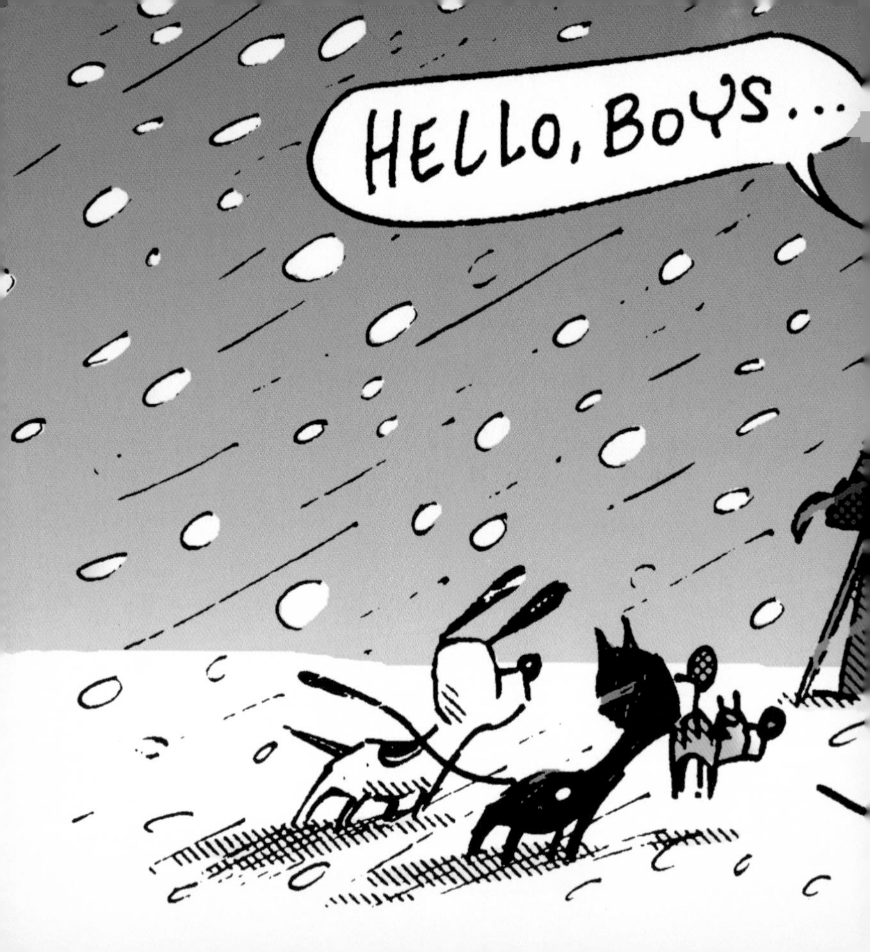
HELLO, BOYS...

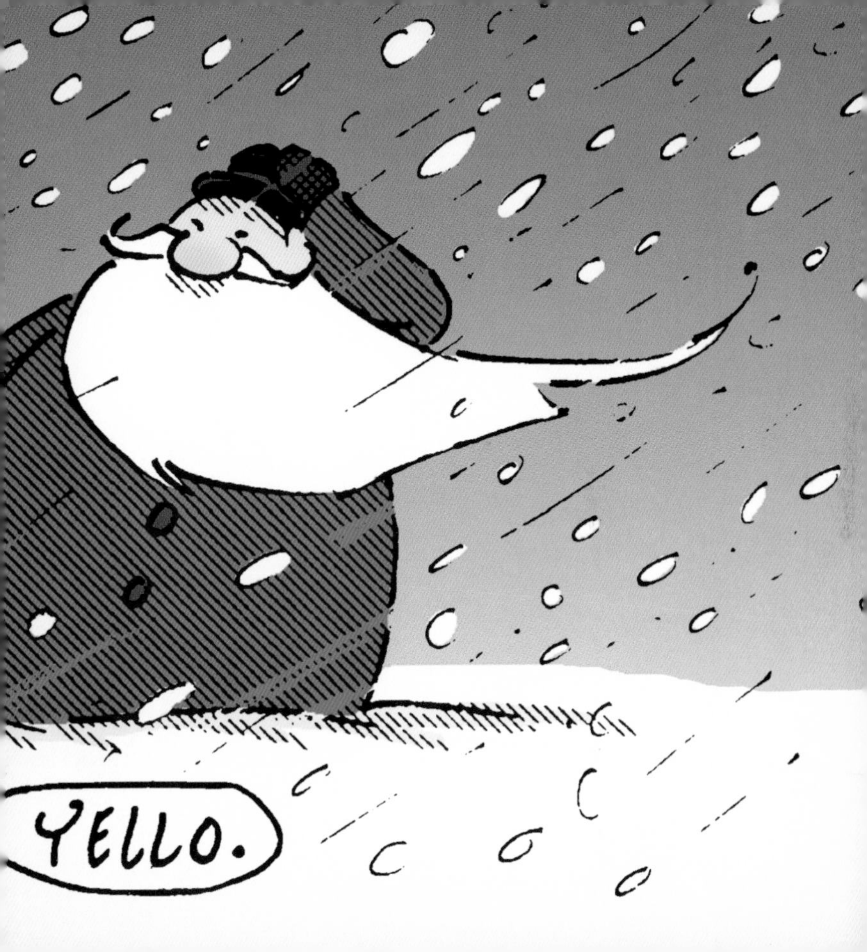
YELLO.

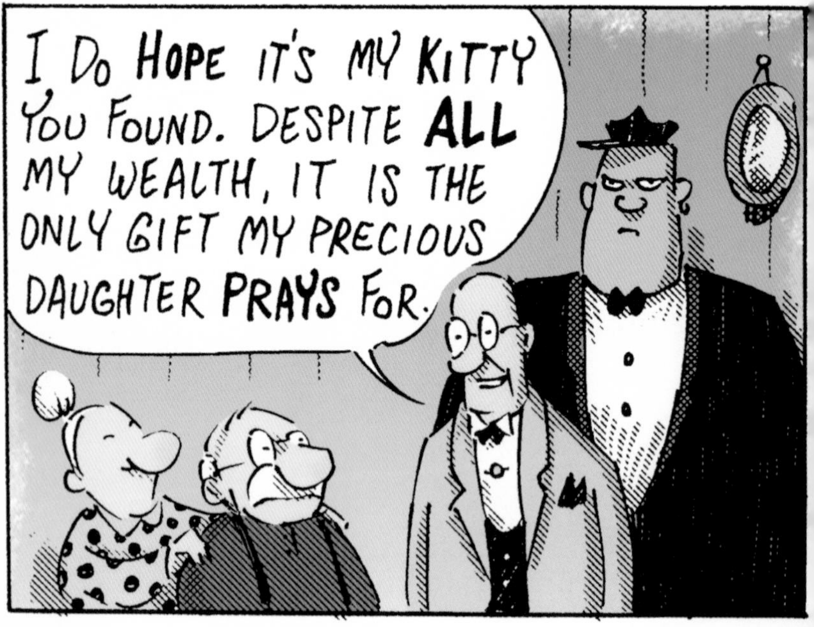
I DO HOPE IT'S MY KITTY YOU FOUND. DESPITE ALL MY WEALTH, IT IS THE ONLY GIFT MY PRECIOUS DAUGHTER PRAYS FOR.

WELL, I'M SURE YOU KNOW, MR. GREY—"MONEY CAN'T BUY LOVE."
ON THE CONTRARY...
ONE CAN PURCHASE "UNCONDITIONAL" LOVE AT ANY ANIMAL SHELTER FOR A SMALL FEE!

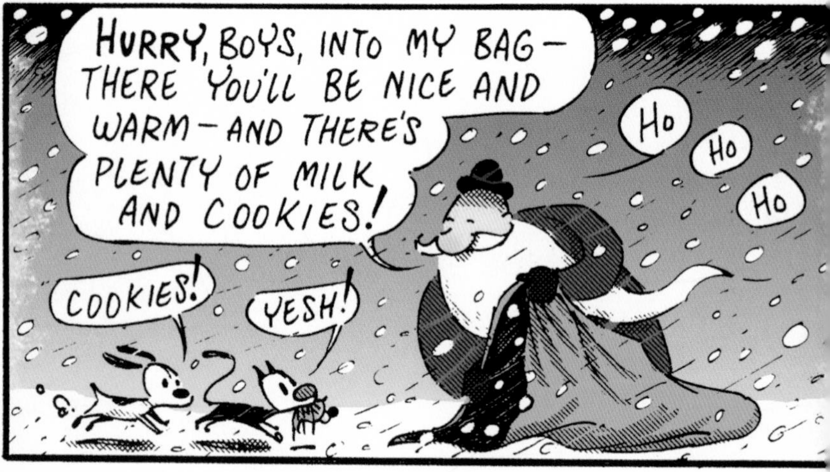
HURRY, BOYS, INTO MY BAG— THERE YOU'LL BE NICE AND WARM—AND THERE'S PLENTY OF MILK AND COOKIES!
Ho
Ho
Ho
COOKIES!
YESH!

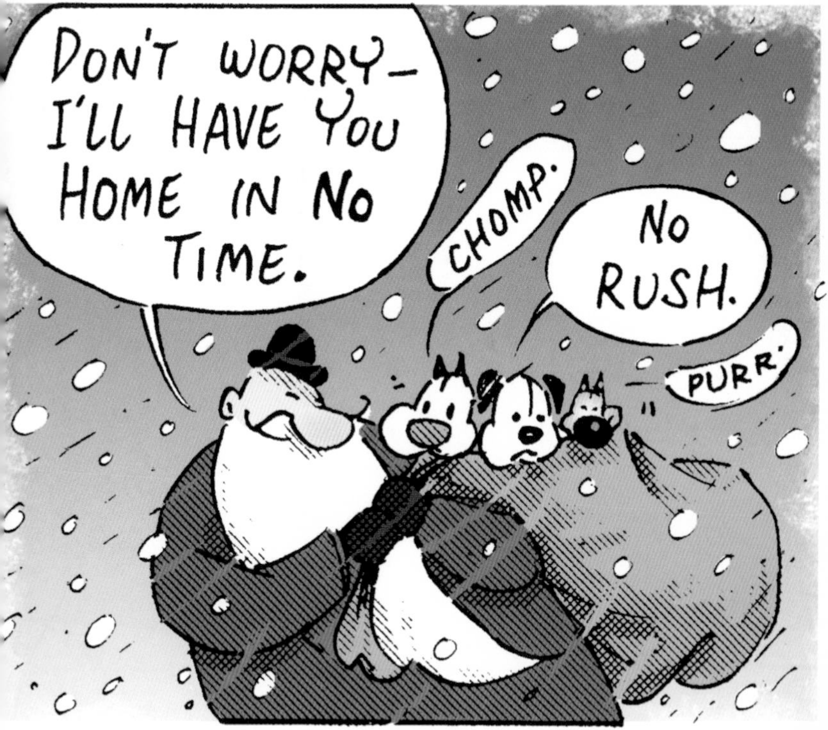
DON'T WORRY–
I'LL HAVE YOU
HOME IN NO
TIME.
CHOMP.
NO
RUSH.
PURR.

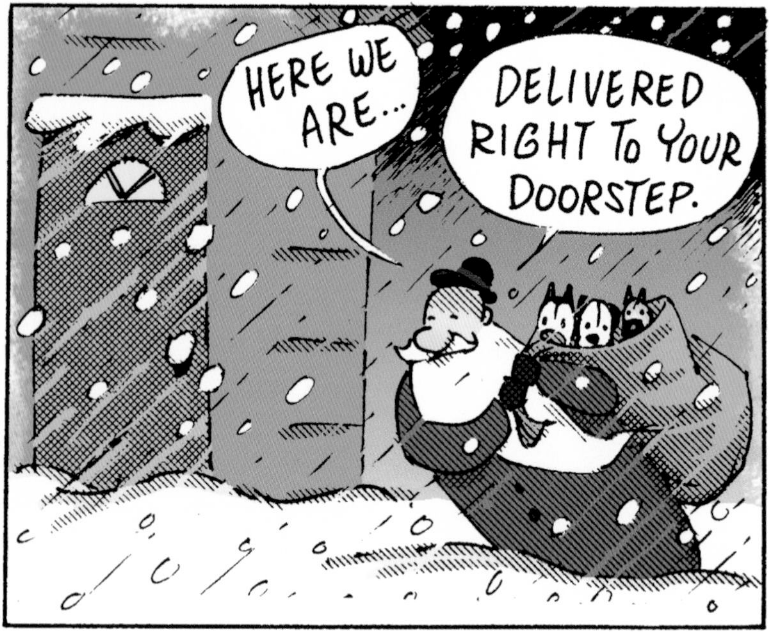
HERE WE ARE...
DELIVERED RIGHT TO YOUR DOORSTEP.

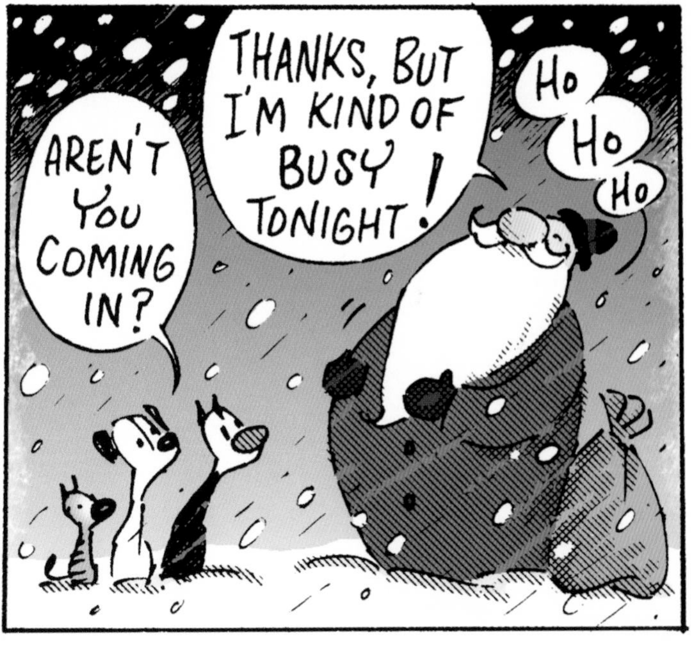
AREN'T YOU COMING IN?
THANKS, BUT I'M KIND OF BUSY TONIGHT!
HO HO HO

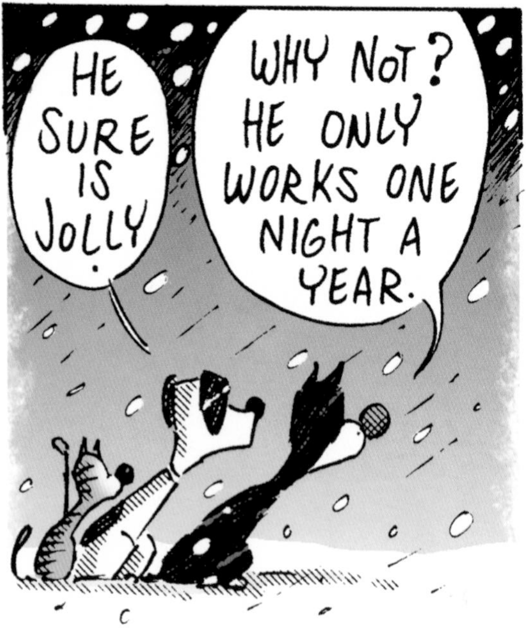
HE SURE IS JOLLY.
WHY NOT? HE ONLY WORKS ONE NIGHT A YEAR.

I'M SURE WE'LL FIND YOUR KITTEN, MR. GREY, BUT... WHAT'S THAT AT THE DOOR...
?

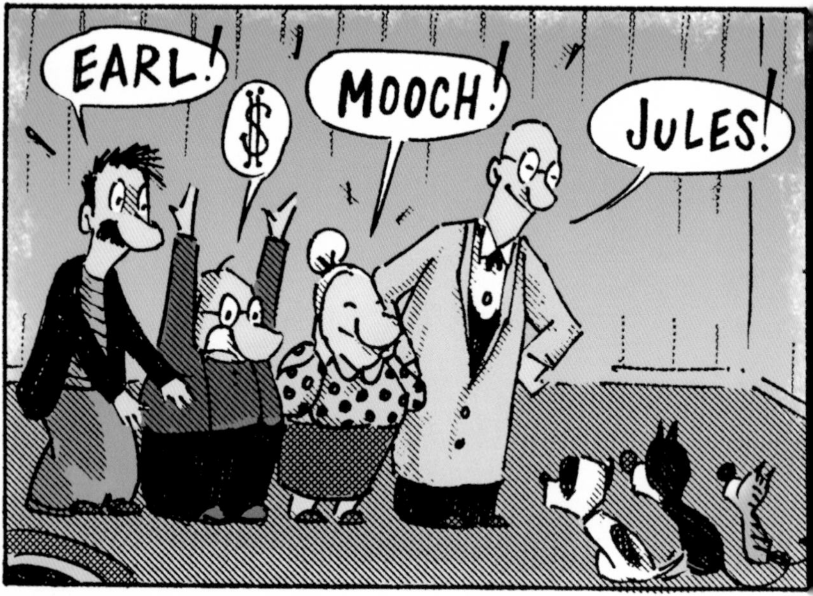
EARL!
$
MOOCH!
JULES!

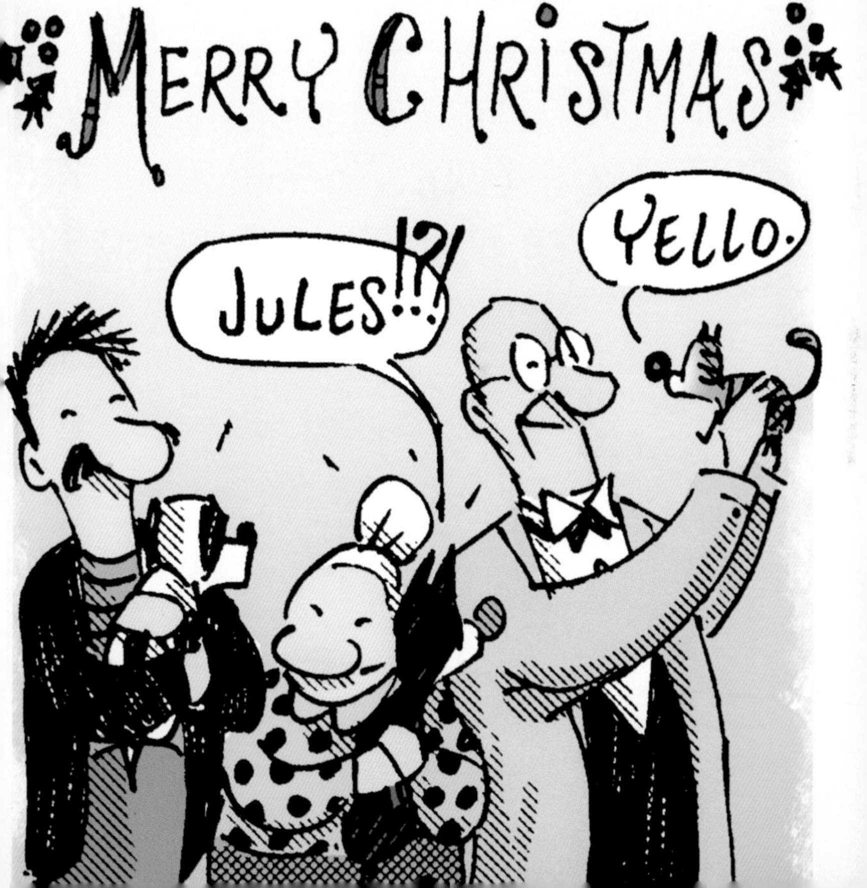
MERRY CHRISTMAS
JULES!!?!
YELLO.

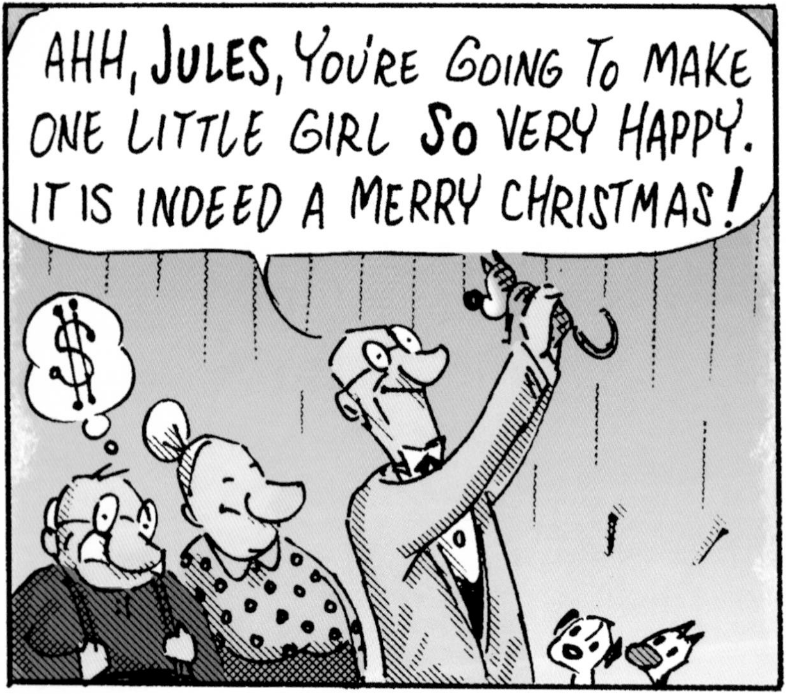
AHH, JULES, YOU'RE GOING TO MAKE ONE LITTLE GIRL SO VERY HAPPY. IT IS INDEED A MERRY CHRISTMAS!
$

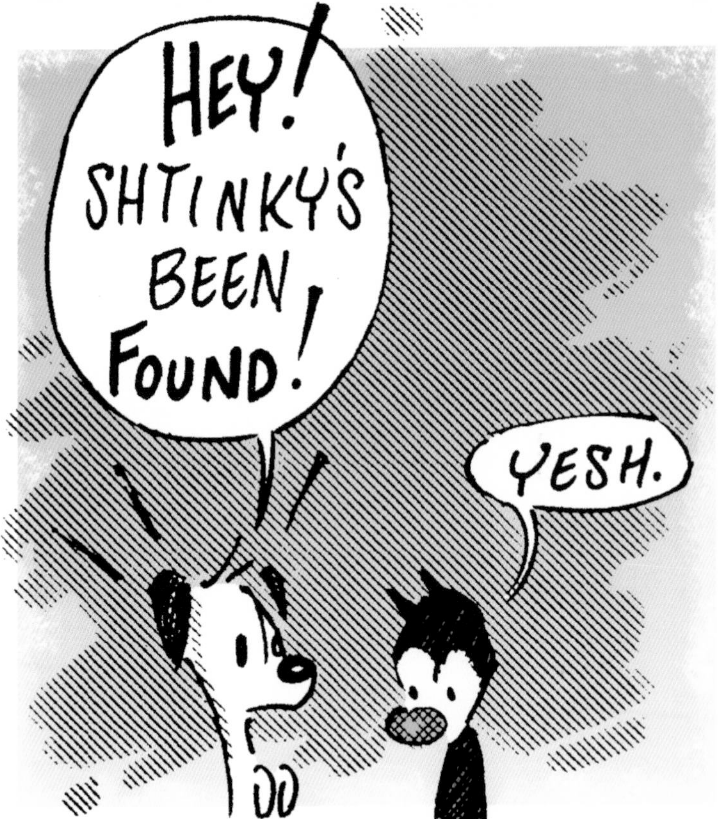
HEY! SHTINKY'S BEEN FOUND!
YESH.

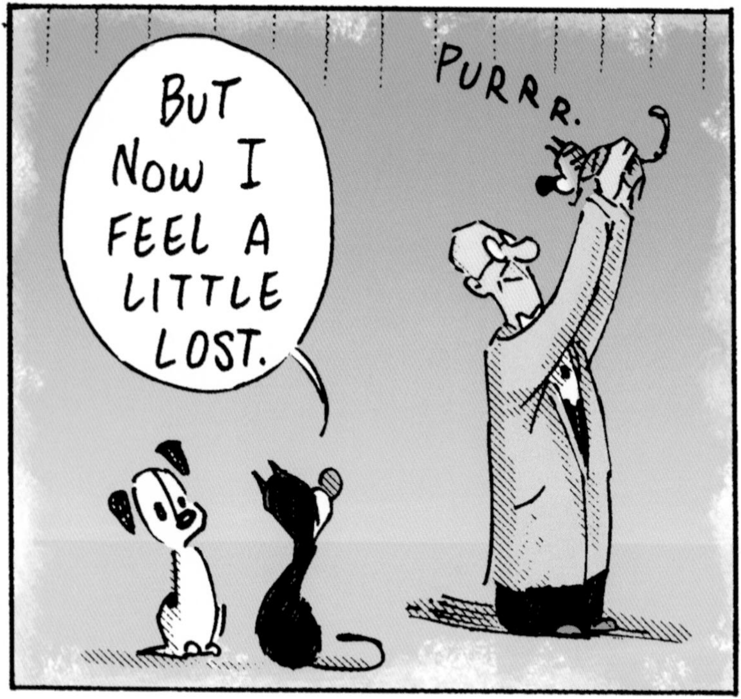
BUT NOW I FEEL A LITTLE LOST.
PURRRR.

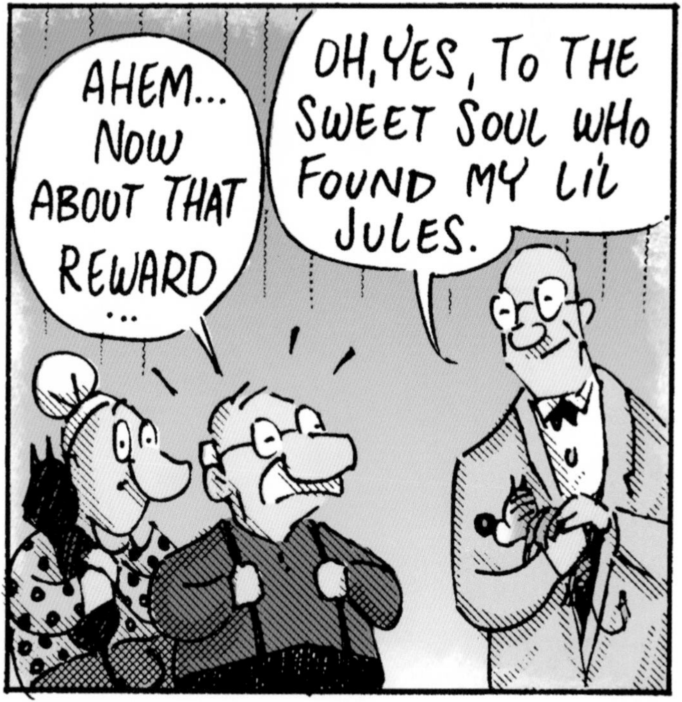
AHEM... NOW ABOUT THAT REWARD ...
OH, YES, TO THE SWEET SOUL WHO FOUND MY LI'L JULES.

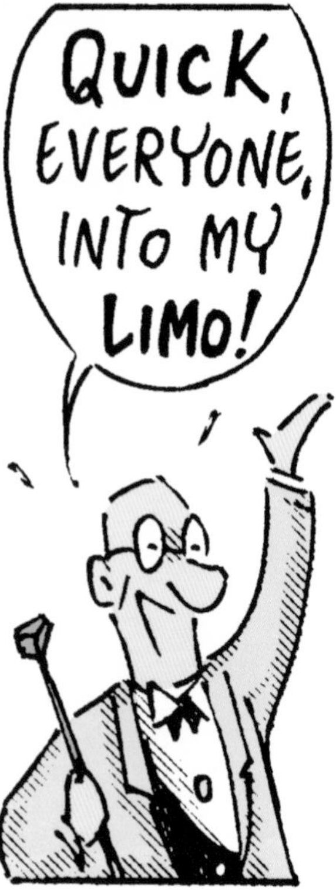
QUICK, EVERYONE, INTO MY LIMO!

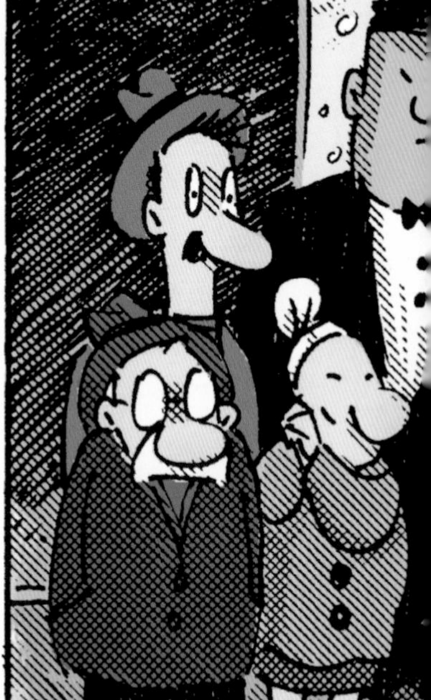

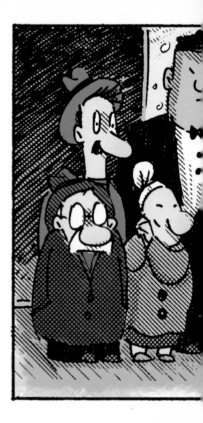

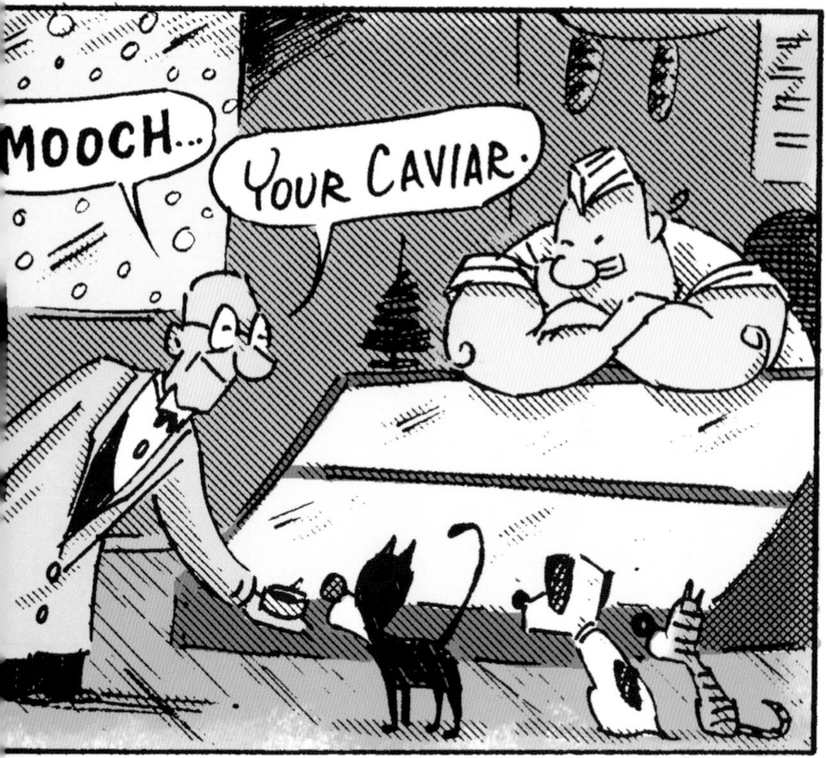
MOOCH...
YOUR CAVIAR.

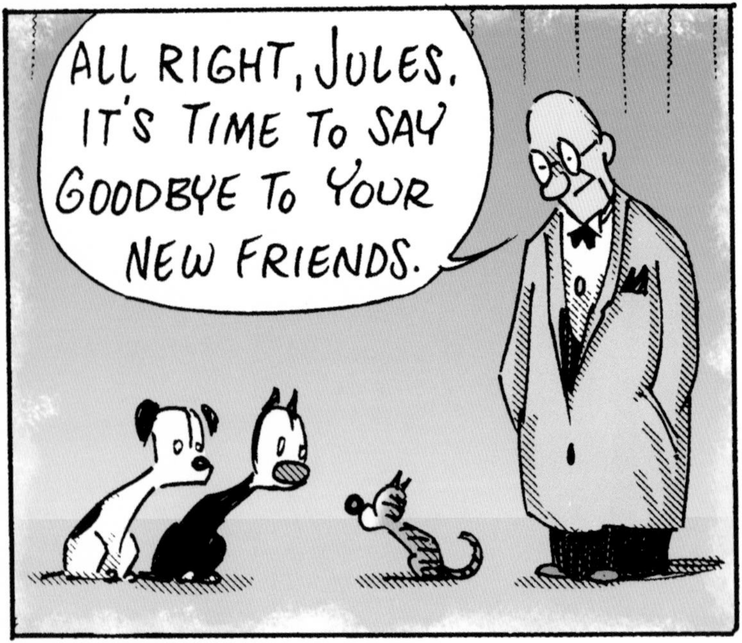
ALL RIGHT, JULES. IT'S TIME TO SAY GOODBYE TO YOUR NEW FRIENDS.

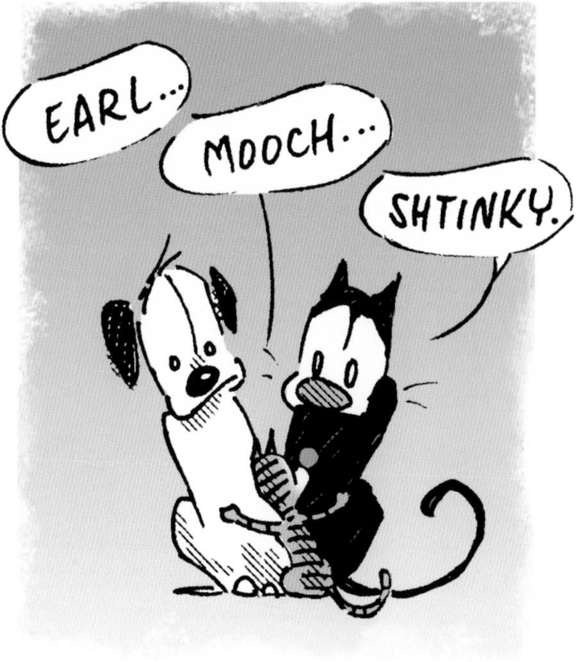
EARL...
MOOCH...
SHTINKY.

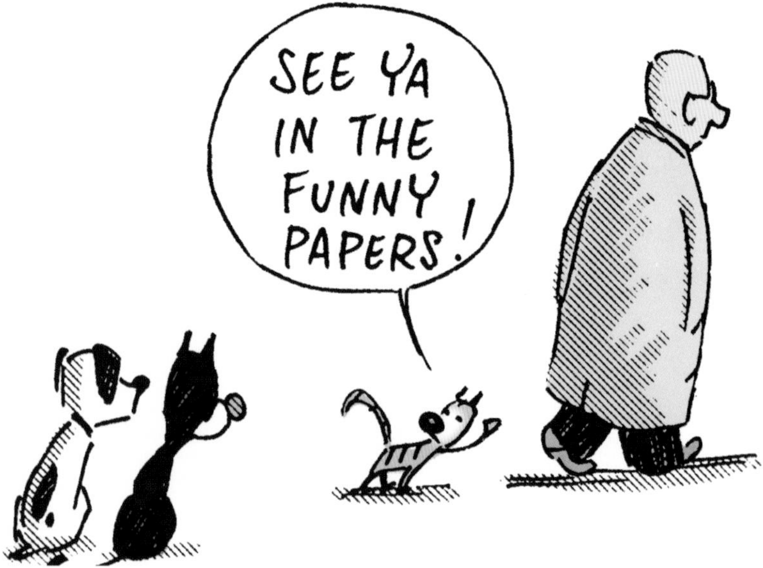
SEE YA IN THE FUNNY PAPERS!